Mothership Connections

To Schubert Ogden
with much gratitude
Gerald West
Sept 2004

SUNY series in Constructive Postmodern Thought

David Ray Griffin, editor

Mothership Connections

A Black Atlantic Synthesis of
Neoclassical Metaphysics
and Black Theology

Theodore Walker Jr.

STATE UNIVERSITY OF NEW YORK PRESS

Published by
STATE UNIVERSITY OF NEW YORK PRESS, ALBANY

© 2004 State University of New York

For information, address State University of New York Press,
90 State Street, Suite 700, Albany, NY 12207

Production, Laurie Searl
Marketing, Anne M. Valentine

Library of Congress Cataloging-in-Publication Data

Walker, Theodore, 1953–
  Mothership connections : a Black Atlantic synthesis of neoclassical metaphysics and Black theology / Theodore Walker, Jr.
    p. cm. — (SUNY series in constructive postmodern thought)
  Includes bibliographical references and index.
  ISBN 0-7914-6089-4 (alk. paper)
    1. Black theology. 2. Metaphysics. 3. Postmodernism. 4. Slavery. I. Title. II. Series.

BT82.7.W345 2004
230'.089'96—dc22
                                                                          2003069331

10   9   8   7   6   5   4   3   2   1

Contents

Preface   vii

Acknowledgments   ix

Series Introduction   xi

Abbreviations   xvii

PART ONE   Modernity in Constructive Postmodern
             and Black Atlantic Views

ONE   Constructive Postmodern Views of Modernity:
        David Ray Griffin, William A. Beardslee,
        Joe Holland, and Frederick Ferré   3

TWO   Black Atlantic Views of Modernity:
        Charles H. Long and Paul Gilroy   9

PART TWO   Neoclassical Metaphysics and Black
             Theology: A Description

THREE   What is Neoclassical Metaphysics?   25

FOUR   What is Black Theology?   37

PART THREE   Neoclassical Metaphysics and Black
              Theology: A Black Atlantic Synthesis

FIVE   Toward a Metaphysics of Struggle   45

SIX   Toward a Metaphysics of Power   53

SEVEN   Toward a Metaphysics of Ethics   61

EIGHT   Epilogue: Toward a Fully Adequate
         Postmodern Theology   69

APPENDIX A   What is Metaphysics?   73

APPENDIX B   What is Theology?   81

         Notes   87

         References   115

         Note on Supporting Center   131

         Index   133

         SUNY series in Constructive Postmodern Thought   145

Preface

With respect to black peoples, "black Atlantic" refers to postslavery black populations and settlements on continents and islands up and down both sides of the Atlantic ocean, and to their various black and colored relations across the whole globe.[1] Black Atlantic populations include black Africans, Afro-Caribbeans, African-Americans (including Afro-North Americans, Afro-South Americans, and Afro-Central Americans), Afro-Europeans, and other hyphenated black Africans. I am an Afro-North American or, less specifically, an African-American.

In this book I offer a black Atlantic contribution to constructive postmodern efforts to understand and transcend modern worldviews and modern world orders.[2] After describing constructive postmodern views of modernity (chapter 1), I offer black Atlantic views of modernity (chapter 2). According to black Atlantic scholars, transatlantic slavery and black Atlantic experiences are major originating, essential, and enduring influences upon modern worldviews and world orders.

Then, I offer a black Atlantic contribution to metaphysics and metaethics. After describing neoclassical metaphysics (chapter 3) and black theology (chapter 4), I draw upon these and other resources to develop a black Atlantic account of metaphysical aspects of struggle (chapter 5), power (chapter 6), and ethical deliberation (chapter 7).

I am very concerned to introduce black Atlantic scholarship to postmodern scholars. Why? Because any adequate account of modernity and its possible transcendence must include sustained analysis of our various connections to transatlantic slavery and black Atlantic experiences. Here the "our" in "our various connections" refers to all modern humans. All humans shaped by modernity are connected to transatlantic slavery and black Atlantic experiences. Constructive postmodern scholars, please meet black Atlantic scholars, especially Charles H. Long, Paul Gilroy, Vincent Harding, and others instructed by W. E. B. Du Bois. Also, please meet black and womanist theologians instructed by black Atlantic thought, including, among others, James H. Cone, Cheryl Townsend Gilkes, and Emilie M. Townes.

I am equally concerned to introduce constructive postmodern metaphysics of the neoclassical and process-relational varieties to black and other liberation theologians. Why? Because no theology or theological ethic can be fully adequate until its metaphysical and metaethical presuppositions are rendered fully explicit, and because, as William R. Jones has shown in his book *Is God a White Racist?*, classical metaphysics yields nonliberating visions of God. Black and other liberation theologians, please meet neoclassical metaphysicians, especially Charles Hartshorne, Schubert M. Ogden, and Franklin I. Gamwell, and constructive postmodern scholars of the process-relational type, especially David Ray Griffin, William A. Beardslee, Joe Holland, Frederick Ferré, Thandeka, John B. Cobb Jr., and others instructed by Alfred North Whitehead.

I am also concerned to render these deliberations accessible to students, including beginning students. Accordingly, the appendix provides novice-friendly introductions to metaphysics (appendix A) and theology (appendix B).

Acknowledgments

I owe almost everything rightly said to the authors of articles and books cited herein. Each citation is an acknowledgment that implies what is explicitly expressed here—gratitude. I am doubly grateful to three of these authors for reading and criticizing my first draft of this book: Joseph L. Allen, Dwight N. Hopkins, and Charles M. Wood. I am triply grateful to two of these authors—Philip E. Devenish and David Ray Griffin—for criticizing several drafts. If the reader could compare the early and penultimate drafts with the book now in hand, she or he would see that the differences are very significant.

For employment and other blessings, including paid research leaves, I am thankful to the Perkins School of Theology at Southern Methodist University in Dallas, Texas. For more day-to-day help than I can itemize, I am thankful to Sue Ferrell, Duane Harbin, Linda Hervey, Shonda Jones, Mary Ann Marshall, Carolyn McCullough, Ann Ralston, Carolyn Santinga, and our associate dean—Marjorie Procter-Smith. For teaching assistance, I am thankful to Sharon Baker and John Wadhams. I am grateful to David R. Brockman for bibliographic research on Du Bois, to John Wallace (Jay) Cole III and Jason E. Vickers for proofreading and criticism, and to Tom Miles for indexing. And for making the literature so readily available, I am thankful to Bridwell Library.

For the essential scholarly gift of regularly scheduled critical dialogue, I am thankful to the students and faculty at the Perkins School of Theology, and to many individuals in the wider Perkins-SMU communities, including the SMU Graduate Program in Religious Studies and the MaGuire Center for Ethics and Public Responsibility. Before coming to Perkins, I served on the faculty at Hood Theological Seminary in Salisbury, North Carolina and at Bethune-Cookman College in

Daytona Beach, Florida. I am thankful to students and faculty at these schools. And I am thankful to the American Academy of Religion, the Center for Process Studies, the Society of Christian Ethics, the Society for the Study of Black Religion, Shiloh Baptist Church in Greensboro, North Carolina, Allen Chapel African Methodist Episcopal Church near Roxboro, North Carolina, and St. Luke "Community" United Methodist Church in Dallas, Texas.

Also, I am thankful to the O'Jays for inspiring attention to Middle Passage experiences with their recording of "Ship Ahoy" (1973) and to George Clinton for inspiring my book title with his recording of "Mothership Connection" (1975).

To these and many others, including especially my father and mother—Theodore D. Walker Sr. (retired minister) and Mary Edna Woods Walker (retired teacher)—"Thank you."

Introduction to SUNY Series in Constructive Postmodern Thought

The rapid spread of the term *postmodern* in recent years witnesses to a growing dissatisfaction with modernity and to an increasing sense that the modern age not only had a beginning but can have an end as well.[1] Whereas the word *modern* was almost always used until quite recently as a word of praise and as a synonym for *contemporary*, a growing sense is now evidenced that we can and should leave modernity behind—in fact, that we *must* if we are to avoid destroying ourselves and most of the life on our planet.

Modernity, rather than being regarded as the norm for human society toward which all history has been aiming and into which all societies should be ushered—forcibly if necessary—is instead increasingly seen as an aberration. A new respect for the wisdom of traditional societies is growing as we realize that they have endured for thousands of years and that, by contrast, the existence of modern civilization for even another century seems doubtful. Likewise, *modernism* as a worldview is less and less seen as The Final Truth, in comparison with which all divergent worldviews are automatically regarded as "superstitious." The modern worldview is increasingly relativized to the status of one among many, useful for some purposes, inadequate for others.

Although there have been antimodern movements before, beginning perhaps near the outset of the nineteenth century with the Romanticists and the Luddites, the rapidity with which the term *postmodern* has become widespread in our time suggests that the antimodern sentiment is more extensive and intense than before, and also that it includes the sense that modernity can be successfully overcome only by going beyond it, not by attempting to return to a premodern form of existence. Insofar as a common element is found in the various ways in which the term is used, *postmodernism* refers to a diffuse sentiment rather than to any common set of doctrines—the sentiment that humanity can and must go beyond the modern.

Beyond connoting this sentiment, the term *postmodern* is used in a confusing variety of ways, some of them contradictory to others. In artistic and literary circles, for example, postmodernism shares in this general sentiment but also involves a specific reaction against modernism in the narrow sense of a movement in artistic-literary circles in the late nineteenth and early twentieth centuries. Postmodern architecture is very different from postmodern literary criticism. In some circles, the term *postmodern* is used in reference to that potpourri of ideas and systems sometimes called "new age metaphysics," although many of these ideas and systems are more premodern than postmodern. Even in philosophical and theological circles, the term *postmodern* refers to two quite different positions, one of which is reflected in this series. Each position seeks to transcend both *modernism*, in the sense of the worldview that has developed out of the seventeenth-century Galilean-Cartesian-Baconian-Newtonian science, and *modernity*, in the sense of the world order that both conditioned and was conditioned by this worldview. But the two positions seek to transcend the modern in different ways.

Closely related to literary-artistic postmodernism is a philosophical postmodernism inspired variously by physicalism, Ludwig Wittgenstein, Martin Heidegger, a cluster of French thinkers—including Jacques Derrida, Michel Foucault, Gilles Deleuze, and Julia Kristeva— and certain features of American pragmatism.[2] By the use of terms that arise out of particular segments of this movement, it can be called *deconstructive, relativistic,* or *eliminative* postmodernism. It overcomes the modern worldview through an antiworldview, deconstructing or even entirely eliminating various concepts that have generally been thought necessary for a worldview, such as self, purpose, meaning, a real world, givenness, reason, truth as correspondence, universally valid norms, and divinity. While motivated by ethical and emancipatory concerns, this type of postmodern thought tends to issue in relativism. Indeed, it seems to many thinkers to imply nihilism.[3] It could, paradoxically, also be called *ultramodernism,* in that its eliminations result from carrying certain modern premises—such as the sensationist doctrine of perception, the mechanistic doctrine of nature, and the

resulting denial of divine presence in the world—to their logical conclusions. Some critics see its deconstructions or eliminations as leading
to self-referential inconsistencies, such as "performative self-contra-
dictions" between what is said and what is presupposed in the saying.

The postmodernism of this series can, by contrast, be called *revisionary, constructive,* or—perhaps best—*reconstructive.* It seeks to overcome
the modern worldview not by eliminating the possibility of worldviews (or "metanarratives") as such, but by constructing a postmodern
worldview through a revision of modern premises and traditional concepts in the light of inescapable presuppositions of our various modes
of practice. That is, it agrees with deconstructive postmodernists that a
massive deconstruction of many received concepts is needed. But its
deconstructive moment, carried out for the sake of the presuppositions
of practice, does not result in self-referential inconsistency. It also is not
so totalizing as to prevent reconstruction. The reconstruction carried
out by this type of postmodernism involves a new unity of scientific,
ethical, aesthetic, and religious intuitions (whereas poststructuralists
tend to reject all such unitive projects as "totalizing modern metanarratives"). While critical of many ideas often associated with modern science, it rejects not science as such but rather that scientism in which
only the data of the modern natural sciences are allowed to contribute
to the construction of our public worldview.

The reconstructive activity of this type of postmodern thought is not
limited to a revised worldview. It is equally concerned with a postmodern world that will both support and be supported by the new
worldview. A postmodern world will involve postmodern persons,
with a postmodern spirituality, on the one hand, and a postmodern
society, ultimately a postmodern global order, on the other. Going
beyond the modern world will involve transcending its individualism,
anthropocentrism, patriarchy, economism, consumerism, nationalism,
and militarism. Reconstructive postmodern thought provides support
for the ethnic, ecological, feminist, pacifist, and other emancipatory
movements of our time, while stressing that the inclusive emancipa-
tion must arise from the destructive features of modernity itself. However, the term *postmodern,* by contrast with *premodern,* is here meant to
emphasize that the modern world has produced unparalleled
advances, as critical theorists have emphasized, which must not be
devalued in a general revulsion against modernity's negative features.

From the point of view of deconstructive postmodernists, this reconstructive postmodernism will seem hopelessly wedded to outdated

concepts because it wishes to salvage a positive meaning not only for the notions of selfhood, historical meaning, reason, and truth as correspondence, which were central to modernity, but also for notions of divinity, cosmic meaning, and an enchanted nature, which were central to premodern modes of thought. From the point of view of its advocates, however, this revisionary postmodernism is not only more adequate to our experience but also more genuinely postmodern. It does not simply carry the premises of modernity through to their logical conclusions, but criticizes and revises those premises. By virtue of its return to organicism and its acceptance of nonsensory perception, it opens itself to the recovery of truths and values from various forms of premodern thought that had been dogmatically rejected, or at least restricted to "practice," by modern thought. This reconstructive postmodernism involves a creative synthesis of modern and premodern truths and values.

This series does not seek to create a movement so much as to help shape and support an already existing movement convinced that modernity can and must be transcended. But in light of the fact that those antimodern movements that arose in the past failed to deflect or even retard the onslaught of modernity, what reasons are there for expecting the current movement to be more successful? First, the previous antimodern movements were primarily calls to return to a premodern form of life and thought rather than calls to advance, and the human spirit does not rally to calls to turn back. Second, the previous antimodern movements either rejected modern science, reduced it to a description of mere appearances, or assumed its inadequacy in principle. They could, therefore, base their calls only on the negative social and spiritual effects of modernity. The current movement draws on natural science itself as a witness against the adequacy of the modern worldview. In the third place, the present movement has even more evidence than did previous movements of the ways in which modernity and its worldview *are* socially and spiritually destructive. The fourth and probably most decisive difference is that the present movement is based on the awareness that *the continuation of modernity threatens the very survival of life on our planet.* This awareness, combined with the growing knowledge of the interdependence of the modern worldview with the militarism, nuclearism, patriarchy, global apartheid, and ecological devastation of the modern world, is providing an unprecedented impetus for people to see the evidence for a postmodern worldview and to envisage postmodern ways of relating to each other, the rest of nature, and the cosmos as a whole. For these reasons, the failure of the previous antimodern movements says little about the possible success of the current movement.

Advocates of this movement do not hold the naively utopian belief that the success of this movement would bring about a global society of universal and lasting peace, harmony and happiness, in which all spiritual problems, social conflicts, ecological destruction, and hard choices would vanish. There is, after all, surely a deep truth in the testimony of the world's religions to the presence of a transcultural proclivity to evil deep within the human heart that no new paradigm, combined with a new economic order, new child-rearing practices, or any other social arrangements, will suddenly eliminate. Furthermore, it has correctly been said that "life is robbery": a strong element of competition is inherent within finite existence, which no social-political-economic-ecological order can overcome. These two truths, especially when contemplated together, should caution us against unrealistic hopes.

No such appeal to universal constants, however, should reconcile us to the present order as if it were thereby uniquely legitimated. The human proclivity to evil in general, and to conflictual competition and ecological destruction in particular, can be greatly exacerbated or greatly mitigated by a world order and its worldview. Modernity exacerbates it about as much as imaginable. We can therefore envision, without being naively utopian, a world order with a far less dangerous trajectory than the one we now have.

This series, making no pretense of neutrality, is dedicated to the success of this movement toward a postmodern world.

DAVID RAY GRIFFIN
SERIES EDITOR

Abbreviations

AA   *Africans in America,* Charles Johnson, Patricia Smith, and the WGBH Research Team

AI   *Adventures of Ideas,* Alfred North Whitehead

AMC   *Alpha: The Myths of Creation,* Charles H. Long

AMEZ   *The African Methodist Episcopal Zion Church,* Bishop William J. Walls

APMH   *Africa—Its Place in Modern History,* W. E. B. Du Bois

BA   *The Black Atlantic,* Paul Gilroy

BB   *Benjamin Banneker,* Charles A. Cerami

BC   *The Black Church in the African American Experience,* C. Eric Lincoln and Lawrence H. Mamiya

BRBR   *Black Religion and Black Radicalism,* Gayraud S. Wilmore

BTBP   *Black Theology and Black Power,* James H. Cone

BTL   *Black Theology of Liberation,* James H. Cone

BV   *Being and Value,* Frederick Ferré

CN   *The Concept of Nature,* Alfred North Whitehead

CP   *The Color Purple,* Alice Walker

CPA   *Christ in a Pluralistic Age,* John B. Cobb Jr.

CSPM   *Creative Synthesis and Philosophic Method,* Charles Hartshorne

DG   *The Divine Good,* Franklin I. Gamwell

DL   *The Darkness and the Light,* Charles Hartshorne

DR   *Divine Relativity,* Charles Hartshorne

EA   *Existence and Actuality,* John B. Cobb Jr. and Franklin I. Gamwell, eds.

ES   *Embracing the Spirit,* Emilie M. Townes, ed.

ESP   *Essays in Science and Philosophy,* Alfred North Whitehead

FF   *Faith and Freedom,* Schubert M. Ogden

GO   *God of the Oppressed,* James H. Cone
GRPW   *God and Religion in the Postmodern World,* David Ray Griffin
IG   *In the Image of God,* David Brion Davis
IGWR   *Is God a White Racist?,* William R. Jones
JP   *Jefferson's Pillow,* Roger Wilkins
LBB   *Life of Benjamin Banneker,* Silvio A. Bedini
LC   *Love and Conflict,* Joseph L. Allen
LE   *The Logic of Evangelism,* William J. Abraham
LP   *Logic of Perfection,* Charles Hartshorne
LW   *Learning to be White,* Thandeka
MBMF   *My Bondage and My Freedom,* Frederick Douglass
MP   *Moral Progress,* Lisa Bellantoni
MVG   *Man's Vision of God,* Charles Hartshorne
OOTM   *Omnipotence and Other Theological Mistakes,* Charles Hartshorne
OT   *On Theology,* Schubert M. Ogden
PE   *Process Ethics,* James R. Gray
PPP   *Postmodernism and Public Policy,* John B. Cobb Jr.
PPS   *Parapsychology, Philosophy, and Spirituality,* David Ray Griffin
PT   *Process Theology,* Ewart H. Cousins, ed.
PUST   *Physics and the Ultimate Significance of Time,* David Ray Griffin
RSN   *Religion and Scientific Naturalism,* David Ray Griffin
RSP   *Reality as Social Process,* Charles Hartshorne
RSPP   *The Reenchantment of Science: Postmodern Proposals,* David Ray
        Griffin, ed.
SMW   *Science and the Modern World,* Alfred North Whitehead
SS   *A Singing Something,* Karen Baker-Fletcher
SSPV   *Spirituality and Society: Postmodern Visions,* David Ray Griffin, ed.
ST   *Slave Testimony,* John W. Blassingame
TCP   "Two Conceptions of Power," Bernard Loomer
TD   *Trouble Don't Last Always,* Evelyn L. Parker
TMS   *A Troubling in My Soul,* Emilie M. Townes, ed.
TR   *There is a River,* Vincent Harding
TST   *The Slave Trade,* Hugh Thomas
VPT   *Varieties of Postmodern Theology,* David Ray Griffin, William A.
        Beardslee, and Joe Holland
WA   *The World and Africa,* W. E. B. Du Bois
WL   *Why Lord?,* Anthony B. Pinn
ZF   *The Zero Fallacy,* Charles Hartshorne

Part I

Modernity in Constructive Postmodern and Black Atlantic Views

1

Constructive Postmodern Views of Modernity: David Ray Griffin, William A. Beardslee, Joe Holland, and Frederick Ferré

What is modernity? According to the black Atlantic scholarship instructed by Paul Gilroy and Charles H. Long (more about Gilroy and Long in chapter 2), one of the most distinguishing features of modernity has been the increasing commodification of creation, such that tens of millions of humans have had the distinctively modern experience of becoming a commodity, a private property purchased for utility and profit via free market transactions and shipped as cargo across the Atlantic ocean. This is not the usual scholarly view of modernity, not even among postmodern scholars.

David Ray Griffin

In the introduction to each of the books in the SUNY series in Constructive Postmodern Thought, series editor Griffin says, "postmodernism refers to a diffuse sentiment rather than to any common set of doctrines—the sentiment that humanity can and must go beyond the modern." For Griffin, *modernism* is the worldview "developed out of the seventeenth century Galilean-Cartesian-Baconian-Newtonian science," and *modernity* is "the world order that both conditioned and was conditioned by this worldview" (RSPP, x; VPT, xii).

Modern worldviews support and are supported by destructive aspects of modern existence. Griffin identifies some of modernity's destructive aspects in saying, "Going beyond the modern world will involve transcending its individualism, anthropocentrism, patriarchy, mechanization, economism, consumerism, nationalism, and militarism" (RSPP, xi; VPT, xiii). "Imperialism" and "nuclearism" are also named as destructive aspects of modernity supported by modern theism (GRPW, 132).[1] Griffin says contemporary postmodern movements differ most decisively from previous antimodern movements on account of present awareness that *"the continuation of modernity threatens the very survival of life on our planet"* (RSPP, xi; VPT, xiii).[2] Accordingly, postmodernism sees an urgent need to "go beyond the modern" (RSPP, x; VPT, xii).

Going beyond the modern includes going beyond modern theology. Postmodernism includes postmodern theology. Concerning modern theology, Griffin says:

Modern theology, it can be agreed, sought to articulate the essence of the biblical faith in a *context* in which the general cultural consciousness was assumed to be shaped by the *modern worldview*, and in which a *rational, objective approach to reality*, through the natural and social sciences, was assumed to support the modern worldview. The varieties of *modern theology* represented different strategies for *"doing theology" within that context*, which at first glance seemed to make theology impossible. (VPT, 1–2)

Modern theology adjusted to the context of modernity, especially to modern scientific views of the world. Going beyond the modern includes going beyond modern theological adjustments to modernity.[3]

In *Varieties of Postmodern Theology*, coauthored with William A. Beardslee and Joe Holland, Griffin identifies four basic types of postmodern theology, with two versions of each type. The four basic types of postmodern theology are "(1) constructive (or revisionary), (2) deconstructive (or eliminative), (3) liberationist, and (4) restorationist (or conservative)" (VPT, 3). Each type seeks to overcome "that noble and flawed enterprise called modern theology," but they differ significantly in their approaches (VPT, 1).

Griffin, Beardslee, and Holland favor the constructive type of postmodern theology. One version of constructive postmodern theology is instructed by the philosophies of Alfred North Whitehead (1861–1947) and Charles Hartshorne (1897–2000). Another version is instructed by the philosophy of Pierre Teilhard de Chardin (1881–1955). Griffin and Beardslee are Whiteheadian. Holland is Teilhardian.

The constructive type of postmodern theology is, says Griffin, "the specifically theological dimension of the constructive postmodern thought to which this series is devoted" (VPT, 3). The constructive postmodernism to which the SUNY series is devoted "seeks to overcome the modern worldview . . . by constructing a postmodern worldview . . . a creative synthesis of modern and premodern truths and values" (VPT, xii–xiii). In accordance with this general constructive postmodern approach to all modern studies, a constructive postmodern approach to theological studies seeks to overcome the errors and inadequacies of modern theology by constructing a postmodern theology.

A similar view of modernity and postmodernism is presented by Beardslee and Holland.

William A. Beardslee

In "Christ In The Postmodern Age: Reflections Inspired by Jean-Francois Lyotard" (VPT, Chapter 4),[4] Beardslee distinguishes between narrow and broad senses of "modern." The narrow sense refers to early twentieth-century art and culture. The broader sense "refers to the period begun by Galileo, Descartes, and Newton, a period that continued into the nineteenth-century rationalism and scientism which are still so influential today" (VPT, 63). Beardslee identifies the "deterministic model of reality" derived from "Newtonian science" as the "single most pervasive factor" of the modern age (VPT, 64). Accordingly, the broad sense of postmodern means "breaking away from the determinism of the modern worldview" (VPT, 64).

Joe Holland

In "The Postmodern Paradigm and Contemporary Catholicism" (VPT, chapter 2), Holland identifies four stages in the historical development of Western culture: "primal, classical, modern, and postmodern" (VPT, 25, 98–108). Concerning the modern stage, he says, "The modern world as a coherent period of social history began seminally with the sixteenth century, matured after the eighteenth century, and now in the late twentieth century is coming to an end" (VPT, 10).

According to Holland, "the destructive side" of modernity became clear "[o]nly in the twentieth century" (VPT, 11). Holland identifies World War I as "the first major expression" of modernity's clearly destructive side, and he identifies the rise of capitalist and socialist totalitarian states, Nazi genocide, and World War II as subsequent twentieth-century expressions of that destructive side (VPT, 11). Other more recent expressions of modernity's destructive side identified by Holland include ecological, sociological, and nuclear destruction, poverty (including the creation of a "structural underclass"), and "deepening secularization" (VPT, 11–12). Holland concludes:

> Thus, we see the negative climax of the modern scientific promise of freedom and progress: even more destructive wars, threats of nuclear annihilation, genocide, totalitarianism, ecological poisoning, erosion of community, marginalization of the poor, and public suppression of religious Mystery. . . . What emerged in the eighteenth century as a bold dream converts itself dialectically in the late twentieth century into a frightening nightmare. This is the cultural end of the modern world. . . . (VPT, 12)

The destructive side of modernity requires a search for a "postmodern vision" (VPT, 18). Holland perceives "postmodern patterns" and a postmodern paradigm "emerging in the praxis" of the Catholic Church (VPT, 19, 22–23).[5]

Frederick Ferré

In contrast to the theological varieties of postmodern thought identified by Griffin in *Varieties of Postmodern Theology*, some varieties of postmodern thought are not theological. To be sure, there is a non-theological version of constructive postmodern metaphysics in the SUNY series in constructive postmodern thought edited by Griffin—Frederick Ferré's *Being and Value: Toward a Constructive Postmodern Metaphysics*.

While not affirming or denying the existence of God, Ferré views modernity in ways similar to constructive postmodern theologians such as Griffin, Beardslee, and Holland. For Ferré, the founders and shapers of modernity were philosophers, logicians, mathematicians, astronomers, and other kinds of scientists, inventors, and technologial innovators (BV).[6] According to Ferré, the "influence of modern science" distinguished "European technologies" from other technologies, and "such new technologies have in turn transformed large portions of our world into what is sometimes, by extension, called *modern scientific civilization*" (SSPV, 133). Modernity's most distinguishing feature is the influence of modern science and science-based technologies.[7]

Theological and nontheological varieties of constructive postmodernism view modernity with major emphasis upon the influences of science, especially "seventeenth century Galilean-Cartesian-Baconian-Newtonian science" (RSPP, x; VPT, xii). I present a different view of modernity in the next chapter.[8]

2

Black Atlantic Views of Modernity: Charles H. Long and Paul Gilroy

Charles H. Long and Middle Passage Cargo

Among black theologies offering a different account of modernity are those instructed by historian of religions Charles H. Long.[1] Long sees the transatlantic slave trade as "the main event" of modernity.

From the fifteenth to the nineteenth centuries, modern North Atlantic maritime nations participated in hugely profitable slave trading.[2] Profits from early modern "free trade" agreements and practices (including "free market" exchanges of commodities, money, and debt) encouraged the purchase and shipment of millions of commodified humans. The numbers of people shipped as cargo from Africa during this period are counted in tens of millions. Estimates range from a low of eleven to twelve million to a high of fifty million.[3] Whether fifty, twenty-five, twelve, or eleven million, this was "the greatest forced migration in human history" (IG, 162). Moreover, the transatlantic slave trading system facilitated the enslavement of many more millions of blacks born into New World slavery. Thus, Long identifies transatlantic slavery as "the main event" that distinguished modern history from previous history.

The main events of modernity included the commodification of African and Native American humans and lands, and related colonial activities. Accordingly, overcoming modernism means overcoming the worldview shared by slave traders, slaveholders, and others who

9

profited from modern economic-social relations. Long argues that contemporary social and ethical inquiry should begin with an analysis of our various connections to commodified human cargo on slave ships during the Middle Passage.

The term *Middle Passage* refers to the transatlantic crossing from Africa to the Americas experienced by commodified human cargo en route to New World slavery. Many slave-trading ships traveled in a triangular pattern with three main passages. Starting in England, the first passage transported manufactured goods to West Africa. The second passage brought human cargo to the Americas. The third passage was a return to England with American raw materials. The second or "middle" passage is described in these words:

> As if two simple words could contain the horror, the journey was called the Middle Passage. It was the nightmarish middle leg of a triad that had its beginning and end in England. From English ports, ships loaded with manufactured goods set off for Africa where the goods were traded for humans. The human cargo was transported to the Americas and traded for raw materials to be sold in England. . . . The Atlantic crossing could take as long as ten weeks, though the duration of voyages varied widely depending upon the wind, the weather, and the port of destination. Whatever its length in minutes and hours and days, it was a pilgrimage so hellish it battles description. No words can hold enough horror. (AA, 70–71).[4]

Long teaches that attending to cargo and other material exchange is essential for understanding human relations in general.[5] For understanding modernity, attention to Middle Passage cargo has priority.[6]

The Priority of the Middle Passage in the Formation of African and Other Modern Identities

Long holds that the priority of Middle Passage cargo derives from its formative influence upon modern identities. For example, before transatlantic slavery, there were no peoples calling themselves "African." Prior to transatlantic slavery, peoples on the continent we now call Africa identified themselves by reference to particular tribes and nations (Ashanti, Hausa, Mendi, Yoruba, Zulu, etc.) without adding reference to color (black) or continent (Africa).[7] "Black" and "African" identities were born during the Middle Passage and matured in subsequent years and generations.

Amistad and African Identity

For a specific historical instance of the modern formation of African identity, consider the written witnesses of the commodified human cargo on the slave ship *Amistad*. We can see the birth and development of African identity in the 1840–1842 letters written by Mendi captives (49 male adults, 3 girls, and 1 eleven-year-old boy) whose successful Middle Passage revolt in 1839 led to freedom and return to Mendi Land (in Sierra Leone) in 1842.

Twenty letters by *Amistad* rebels appear in chronological sequence in *Slave Testimony: Two Centuries of Letters, Speeches, Interviews, and Autobiographies*, edited by John W. Blassingame (ST, 30–46). In the earliest letters written in 1840 when the Mendi rebels were still in their first year of learning to read and write in English,[8] they identified themselves as Mendi people from Mendi Land. In subsequent letters written in 1841 and 1842, they added increasingly frequent references to Africa. Finally, in an October 1842 letter written by a formerly enslaved person from a different tribe (A-ku), we are told that free "Mendian Africans" have returned, and that they encountered other formerly enslaved persons from different tribes and nations who were "all Africans" (ST, 45).

For these Mendi and A-ku, African identity came after their Middle Passage experiences as cargo on the *Amistad*. And for other peoples indigenous to the continent we now call Africa, African identity came after colonialism and transatlantic slavery.

Other Modern Identities

The same is true of other modern identities. These other identities include "European," "European-American," "white," "black," "red," "Indian," and "Native American." This color-coded and land-oriented vocabulary, and related theories (especially theories of race, ethnicity, and civilization[9]), emerged in response to transatlantic discovery, conquest, slavery, and colonialism.

Prior to transatlantic slavery, Mendi, A-ku, Hausa, Yoroba, and other peoples from lands along the southeast Atlantic did not identify themselves as "African" or "black." Similarly, Massachuset, Pamlico, Catawba, Waccamaw, and other peoples aboriginal to lands along the northwestern Atlantic did not identify themselves as "Indian," "Native American," or "red." And Portuguese, Spanish, French, British, Dutch,

German, and other peoples from lands along the northeast Atlantic did not identify themselves as "white" or "European."

Where these modern labels are deployed to speak of pre-Middle Passage histories, they are being extended back into time periods when they were not current. Strictly speaking, prior to the Middle Passage, there is no African history as such, no black history as such, no American or Native American history as such, and no white or European history as such.

The priority of the Middle Passage also derives from taking commodification as essential to modernity. According to Long, the increasing commodification of God's creatures and creations describes the historical process leading towards modernity. And modernity became fully actual when tens of millions of commodified humans were being shipped across the Atlantic.

Paul Gilroy and the Black Atlantic World

The priority of the Middle Passage for understanding modern experience is observed in *The Black Atlantic: Modernity and Double Consciousness* (1993) by Paul Gilroy. Gilroy is a black European senior lecturer in sociology at the University of London. Building upon the work of W. E. B. Du Bois (1868–1963), Gilroy concludes that transatlantic slavery "marked out blacks as the first truly modern people" (BA, 221).

Du Bois's concept of "double consciousness" as developed in *The Souls of Black Folk* (1903) is about consciousness of being black and American, and more precisely, being black and a U.S. citizen. Gilroy employs double consciousness in reference to being black and European, and more precisely to being black and a citizen of Britain. Furthermore, Gilroy finds that double consciousness illuminates the experiences of post-slavery populations in general (BA, 126).

Modern slavery was a transatlantic phenomenon that reached up and down both sides of the Atlantic. Modern black experiences are not confined to the U.S., or to North America. There are black post-slavery settlements throughout the American continents (North, Central, and South), the Caribbean islands, and in Europe. Blacks in Europe and elsewhere in "the Atlantic world" share double consciousness and other similarities. Gilroy holds that "the post-slave cultures of the Atlantic world are in some significant way related to one another and to the African cultures from which they partly derive" (BA, 81).

According to Gilroy, there is a "diaspora" of post-slavery black settlements "heuristically called the black Atlantic world" (BA, 3).[10]

Like Long, Gilroy starts his analysis of modernity by focusing on
ships, especially slave ships. He says a ship is "a living micro-cultural,
micro-political system in motion" (BA, 4), and ships "refer us back to
the middle passage, to the half-remembered micropolitics of the slave
trade and its relationship to both industrialisation and modernisation"
(BA, 17). Ships and transatlantic shipping connections were decisive
influences in the formation of the whole modern world, including the
modern black Atlantic world. For understanding the black Atlantic
world, and for understanding the modern world in general, Gilroy
prescribes starting with ships and shipping routes.[11]

Gilroy's account of black maritime experience is not limited to the
Middle Passage experiences of newly enslaved Africans. Even during
slavery, there were other black transatlantic travelers, including free
black passengers, free black sailors, and maritime slaves.[12] Gilroy notes
that "at the end of the eighteenth century a quarter of the British navy
was composed of Africans" (BA, 13), and that one prominent black
transatlantic traveler—Frederick Douglass (1817–1895)—was able to
escape slavery disguised as a sailor because black sailors were a common sight near harbor towns such as Baltimore.

Gilroy draws upon the work of black transatlantic travelers. The well-
traveled Du Bois is foremost among his sources. Other black transatlantic travelers consulted by Gilroy include: Phyllis Wheatley, Martin
Robinson Delany, William Wells Brown, Frederick Douglass, Alexander
Crummel, Anna Julia Cooper, Ida B. Wells Barnett, Marcus Garvey, and
Richard Wright.[13] Gilroy's study of literature by black transatlantic travelers yields "a more ambitious understanding of modernity" (BA, 197).

Here "more ambitious" means more ambitious than postmodern
understandings such as "the minimal definition that identifies the term
[modernity] simply with the consciousness of the novelty of the present"
(BA, 197). Gilroy contrasts his understanding with Jürgen Habermas's
focus on time, time-consciousness, and the novelty of the present.[14] In a
section called "Slavery and The Enlightenment Project," Gilroy observes
that Habermas and other postmodern advocates of the modern Enlightenment project fail to examine slavery's place in modernity. Gilroy says:

If popular writers like Jürgen Habermas and Marshall Berman are to be believed,
the unfulfilled promise of modernity's Enlightenment project remains a belea-
guered but nonetheless vibrant resource which may even now be able to guide

the practice of contemporary social and political struggles. In opposition to this view, I propose that the history of the African diaspora and a reassessment of the relationship between modernity and slavery may require a more complete revision of the terms in which the modernity debates have been constructed than any of its academic participants may be willing to concede. (BA, 46)

Gilroy prescribes reconstructing the history of modernity "from the slaves' points of view" (BA, 55). According to black Atlantic understandings of modernity, the modern world is "fragmented along axes constituted by racial conflict" and "periodised" by reference to the Middle Passage (BA, 197).

A Black Atlantic Critique of Postmodernism

Du Bois pioneered understanding modernity by reference to transatlantic slavery and Africa. In addition to articulating double consciousness in *The Souls of Black Folk* (1903), Du Bois was attentive to slavery in his Harvard doctoral dissertation—*The Suppression of the African Slave-Trade in the United States of America 1638–1870* (1896)—and he was attentive to Africa's place in modernity in *Africa—Its Place in Modern History* (1930) and in *The World and Africa: An Inquiry into the Part Which Africa Has Played in World History* (1947).

Black theologies instructed by Du Bois, Long, and Gilroy share the "more ambitious understanding of modernity" (BA, 197). They see the essential place of Africa in the modern world. And prior to the formation of distinctively modern identities and conceptions (including "civilization," "race," "color," "African," "European," "Oriental," "American," "Native American," "Euro-American," "African-American," "black," "colored," "white," "red," "yellow," "brown," "Negroid," "Caucasoid," "Mongoloid"), they see slave ships on the Atlantic. And they see that black Atlantic experiences and other experiences shaped by connections to transatlantic slavery are constituitive of modernity. According to these instructions, it is not possible to produce an adequate account of modernity without extensive study of our various connections to transatlantic slave trading and black Atlantic experiences.[15]

Contrasting Views of Modernity

Constructive postmodern scholars typically mark the birth of modernity by reference to science. Beardslee says modernity "refers to the period begun by Galileo, Descartes, and Newton" (VPT, 63), and he identifies the "deterministic model of reality" derived from "Newtonian science" as the "single most pervasive factor" of the modern age (VPT, 64). For Holland, the "birth of modern culture, centered in the North Atlantic nations, was midwifed" by mass printing, education, and other influences that "promoted the growth of modern science and technology" (VPT, 102). And Ferré says:

> The secret is no secret. We all know that it was the rise of what we loosely call *science* that changed our world by transforming all technologies, both benign and malignant. The change was literally radical. It entered from the intellectual root by grafting theoretical to practical reason, for the first time in human history. That is, the crucial new factor is thought engaged in exact theory, disciplined by logic and empirical verification. (SS, 135)[16]

Beardslee, Holland, and Ferré hold that the influences of early modern science and science-based technologies gave birth to the early period or "first stage of modernity" (Griffin, SSPV, 144).

Constructive postmodern regard for the influence of Galilean-Cartesian-Baconian-Newtonian science calls attention to the seventeenth century. Griffin says the "modern paradigm" (the worldview and ethic ordering modern lives) has been increasingly dominant "since the seventeenth century" (SSPV, 143). While acknowledging influences from the sixteenth century and earlier (including the Renaissance), constructive postmodern scholars see the modern paradigm becoming fully actual and increasingly dominant in the seventeenth century.[17]

Black Atlantic thought calls for adding a fifteenth-century marker—the August 8, 1444, sale of 235 commodified humans shipped as cargo from Africa by Portugal (TST, 21). This is the earliest known transatlantic slave-trading transaction, and therefore it is an appropriate place to mark the birth of modernity.[18]

For Whitehead and constructive postmodern scholars, modernity is mainly about the influence of modern science, starting in the seventeenth century, "seminally with the sixteenth," says Holland (VPT, 10). For Du Bois and black Atlantic scholars, modernity is also and mainly about the increasing commodification of the world, starting with the emergence of transatlantic slavery in the fifteenth century.

Accordingly, while Whitehead was giving his 1925 Lowell lectures—subsequently published as *Science and the Modern World*—Du Bois was researching *Africa—Its Place in Modern History* (1930). And more recently, while Griffin was editing *The Reenchantment of Science: Postmodern Proposals* (1988), Gilroy was writing lectures that became *The Black Atlantic: Modernity and Double Consciousness* (1993). And while Ferré is identifying "the rise of modern science" as "the secret of modern technology and the modern world" (SSPV, 134–35), Long is asking, "What is the secret of the cargo?"[19]

Black Atlantic scholars, postmodern scholars, and modern scholars all recognize modernity's classical Greek and Roman heritage. Black Atlantic, postmodern, and modern scholars recognize that modern science *and* modern slavery had classical Greek and Roman precursors. Though on a vastly smaller scale, and not instructed by doctrines of black inferiority, slavery was part of the classical Greek and Roman worlds.[20] From a black Atlantic perspective, neither modern nor postmodern thought is sufficiently critical of classical philosophies for authorizing Greek, Roman, and modern slavery.

So far I have been contrasting constructive postmodern views with black Atlantic views by referencing two marks of modernity—science and slavery, or more precisely, modern science and transatlantic slavery. Like modern thought, constructive postmodern thought seldom recognizes slavery as an important mark of modernity. Black Atlantic thought recognizes both science and slavery, and the priority of the latter.

Benjamin Banneker

Declaring a universal human right to liberty while enslaving millions is another distinguishing mark of modernity. Obviously, this is morally duplicitous. Accordingly, in his August 1791 letter to Thomas Jefferson, Benjamin Banneker (1731–1806), a free black gentleman-farmer, astronomer, and almanac publisher, informed the slave-holding author of the Declaration of Independence that he was "guilty of that most criminal act" (denial of liberty) which he "professedly detested in others" (BB, 166).

Banneker's 1791 letter to Jefferson covered a handwritten copy of his 1792 almanac, which included an "ephemeris" of original computations of the varying emphemeral positions of the sun, moon, planets, and stars during the coming year. Because Jefferson had expressed doubts about the mental abilities of black people, Banneker's almanac and ephemeris was offered as "resounding proof that a black—and one with almost no formal education—had actually mastered a subject that only a handful of scholarly whites could tackle" (BB, 162).

Ignoring Banneker's Contributions to Modern Cosmology

In addition to science, slavery, and a morally duplicitious affirmation of liberty, another characteristic mark of modernity is the habit of ignoring black Atlantic contributions to science. Beside frequently neglecting the social scientific work of Du Bois, modern and postmodern accounts of scientific inquiry seldom acknowledge Benjamin Banneker's contributions to astronomy and cosmology.

In *Benjamin Banneker: Surveyor, Astronomer, Publisher, Patriot* (2002), biographer Charles A. Cerami reports that Banneker was an accomplished mathematician and astronomer.[21] Cerami notes that Banneker corrected the miscalculations of two world famous astronomers (BB, 72–74), and that he correctly "believed Sirius [which appears to be a single star] was actually two stars—before the world of astronomy knew this to be so" (BB, 183, 218).[22]

In his 1792 almanac and ephemeris, Banneker offered a fully modern scientific view of our sun, this planet, and the universe. Banneker wrote:

The sun, though seemingly smaller than the dial it illuminates, is abundantly larger than this whole earth, on which so many lofty mountains rise and such vast oceans roll. A girdle formed to go round its circumference would require a length of millions. Were its solid contents to be estimated, the account would overwhelm our understanding and be almost beyond the power of language to express. . . .

This sun, with all its attendant planets, is but a very little part of the grand machine of the universe; every star, though in appearance no bigger than the diamond that glitters upon a lady's ring, is really a vast globe, like the sun in size and in glory; no less spacious, no less luminous, than the radiant source of the day: So that every star is not barely a world, but the centre of a magnificent system; has a retinue of worlds, irradiated by its beams, and revolving arounds its attractive influence, all of which are lost to our sight in unmeasurable wilds of ether. That the stars appear like so many diminutive and scarce distinguishable points is owing to their immense and inconceivable distance. Immense and inconceivable indeed it is, since a ball, shot from a loaded cannon, and flying with unabated rapidity, must travel at this impetuous rate almost seven hundred thousand years, before it could reach the nearest of these twinkling luminaries.

While beholding this vast expanse, I learn my own extreme meanness. I would also discover the abject littleness of all terrestrial things. What is the earth, with all her ostentatious scenes, compared with this astonishing grand furniture of the skys? What but a dim speck, hardly perceivable in the map of the universe? (BB, 223)

Through his almanacs (published from 1791 to 1797), Banneker gave us volumes of original astronomical calculations, and he popularized distinctively modern visions of our sun, of stars as remote suns, many with orbital companions (sometimes other suns, sometimes planets), and of extra-solar planets with intelligent life.[23]

Yet, modern and postmodern accounts of modern science rarely mention Banneker's contributions.[24] Instead, Banneker is better known for his more earthly practical accomplishments—building a wooden clock and doing survey work on the District of Columbia.[25] By failing to acknowledge Banneker's contributions to our cosmological visions, we continue the characteristically modern habit of ignoring black Atlantic contributions to science and the modern world.[26]

Slavery in Constructive Postmodern Thought

Distinguishing "worldview" from "world order" and focusing on "world order" extends the range of postmodern concerns well beyond reconstructing modern scientific worldviews. In the SUNY series in Constructive Postmodern Thought, *The Reenchantment of Science* (1988) focuses mainly on the modern scientific worldview, while *Spirituality and Society: Postmodern Visions* (1988) focuses more on the modern world order/society. In *Spirituality and Society* nine postmodern scholars offer views of modern society that include historical, political, economic, and other social concerns. As indicated in the index, among many others, these concerns include the following: aesthetics, agriculture, bureaucratization, capitalism, communism, culture, democracy, ecological destruction, economics, feminism, freedom, homelessness, industrialization, liberalism, liberation theology, liberty, militarism, nonviolence, peace, sexuality, spirituality, war, witch hunting, and work (SSPV, 157–62), but not slavery.[27]

Slavery is not a major theme in any of the essays in *Spirituality and Society*, and therefore it does not appear in the index. But there is an important mention of slavery where Griffin identifies it as one of the "disastrous" and "destructive consequences" of modern dualistic thinking about "the nature of nature" (SSPV, 146). Griffin says that dualism's "materialistic view of nature" was "a major cause of colonization (including neocolonization), mass enslavement, and war in modern times," and that dualistic ideas were used "to justify the enslavement and even decimation of 'primitives,' in order to allow the 'fully human' Europeans to populate the planet and develop it" (SSPV, 146–47).

Griffin is correct in noting that modern dualism had "destructive consequences" that included justifying colonialism and mass enslavement. Additionally, consider the temporal priority of early transatlantic slavery. Fifteenth- and sixteenth-century slaveholders and slave traders required a worldview that could reconcile their increasing commitment to enslaving others with their increasing commitment to liberty for themselves. This morally duplicitous requirement encouraged the development of dualistic thinking. Then, in the seventeenth century, dualistic worldviews were further developed and widely embraced. And, as Griffin notes, seventeenth-century dualism encouraged the continuation and expansion of slavery and colonialism.

When we analyze modernity without reference to early modern slavery, it appears that modern theory was leading practice. And indeed Ferré says that premodern theory "follows rather than leads practical success," but in the modern era "verifiable theory began to lead technological practice" (SSPV, 135). However, when our analysis includes study of early modern slavery, then we see that early modern practice was a major cause of modern dualistic theory.

Beyond Griffin's brief mention, *Spirituality and Society* includes almost nothing about slavery. Similarly, of ten contributors describing modern society in *Postmodern Politics for a Planet in Crisis* (1993), only Roger Wilkins discusses slavery and "the contemporary burden of its legacies" (158).[28]

From among constructive postmodern scholars, Wilkins, Thandeka, and Cobb are the most attentive to the formative influences of slavery upon modern self-understandings. In *Learning to Be White: Money, Race and God in America* (1999) Thandeka offers an analysis of the construction of white identity that is fully attentive to the influences of slavery. In *Postmodernism and Public Policy: Reframing Religion, Culture, Education, Sexuality, Class, Race, Politics, and the Economy* (2002) Cobb draws upon Thandeka's work and his own heritage as "a Southern white whose ancestors owned slaves" (PPP, 162) to offer a postmodern deliberation on domestic race and class relations. Cobb says:

Until whites recognize how deep is their self-identification as whites, they will not understand the problems they create both for themselves and for those whom they define as not white. The racial problem in the United States must be redefined as that of the social construction of the white race. Until that is deconstructed, there is no possibility for those who have been excluded from whiteness to have equal opportunity. (PPP, 155–56)

Cobb and Thandeka hold that North American white identity developed from the need to justify slavery, and that many European immigrants learned to be white because "their designation as 'white' gave them some protection and hope for the future" (PPP, 157). Attention to the formative influences of slavery favorably distinguishes these works (LW; PPP) from most constructive postmodern accounts of modernity.

Slavery in Black Atlantic Thought

Black theologies are very attentive to slavery, to the experiences of slaves, and to slave religions.[29] And black theologies instructed by black Atlantic scholarship recognize the priority of the Middle Passage for understanding modernity.

In contrast to black theologies, postmodern theologies, like modern theologies, typically grant no priority to the Middle Passage, and they seem not to see slavery, black experiences, or Africa as essential to the modern world. For example, Holland says, "Only in the twentieth century did the destructive side of the modern world become clear," and World War I was "the first major expression" of modernity's clearly destructive side (VPT, 11). Obviously, Holland does not see transatlantic slavery as part of the modern world.

In a section of *The Black Atlantic* called "Slavery and the Enlightenment Project," Gilroy laments the modern scholarly habit of viewing slavery as barely relevant to modernity. He says:

if it is perceived to be relevant at all, the history of slavery is somehow assigned to blacks. It becomes our special property rather than a part of the ethical and intellectual heritage of the West as a whole. (BA, 49)

Black theologies instructed by black Atlantic scholarship emphasize "the intimate association of modernity and slavery" (BA, 53).[30] Typically, modern and postmodern theologies do not share this emphasis.[31]

According to Long, where Middle Passage cargo is given no priority, modernity is not adequately described, and talk of postmodernism is premature. When we try to account for ourselves without references to our many various connections to that human cargo, we are implicitly claiming to be fundamentally untouched by our connections to transatlantic slavery. This is a characteristically modern claim. However, given the formative influences of transatlantic slavery upon modern identities, the claim is clearly untrue.

Slavery and other colonial relations are no less characteristic of modernity than scientific discoveries. The so-called age of discovery was also the age of slavery and colonialism. To be sure, according to Vine Deloria Jr. of the Sioux nations, the very concept of discovery had colonial functions. In Native American experiences, to be "discovered" is to become a colonial property.[32]

Moreover, analyzing economic and other connections to transatlantic slavery reveals that many philosophers and scientists profited from the transatlantic slave-trading economy. Those profits gave many gentlemen scholars the wealth and leisure time needed to pursue their scholarly inquiries.

In *Jefferson's Pillow* (2001) Roger Wilkins shows that the lives of George Washington, George Mason, and Thomas Jefferson were cushioned by slavery. Modern scholars were well connected to the profit-making end of a "free market" global economy largely driven by profits from transatlantic slave trading and slave holding. In addition to being shaped by and receiving benefits from slavery, modern scholars made many original contributions to the justification of slavery and colonialism, including materialistic views of nature (Griffin) and white supremacist theories of race and history (Du Bois).[33]

The effort to get beyond modernity requires understanding it in terms more comprehensive than the influences of modern European science and science-based technology.[34] Most postmodernism suffers from a characteristically modern failure to see the formative influences of transatlantic slavery and black Atlantic experiences.[35] And most postmodern accounts of modernity ignore connections to Middle Passage cargo.

Like most varieties of postmodernism, most postmodern theologies (including most constructive postmodern theologies) draw no connections between modernity and slavery, and no connections between modern Christianity and slavery. By contrast, black theologies instructed by black Atlantic scholarship make these connections. For example, Henry James Young quotes Du Bois as saying modern slavery was "created" and "continued" by Christians.[36] Making these connections is essential to the postmodern work of describing and transcending modernity. Accordingly, the study of black theology is essential to developing a fully adequate postmodern theology.

Part II

Neoclassical Metaphysics
and Black Theology:
A Description

3

What is Neoclassical Metaphysics?

Part One concludes that according to black Atlantic criteria, most constructive postmodern views of modernity are seriously inadequate. Most constructive postmodernism has failed to see that transatlantic slavery, genocide against Native Americans, and other colonial interactions, were among the main originating and distinguishing events of modernity. With respect to this failure, thus far, most postmodernism has not distinguished itself from modernism. *A more adequate account of modernity and its possible transcendence can be achieved by drawing mothership connections,* that is, by outlining our various connections (social, historical, genetic, economic, religious, etc.) to the transatlantic shipments of commodified human cargo that gave birth to modernity.[1]

Mothership connections are essential to a fully adequate postmodern theology. In addition to explicating this essential sociological content, a fully adequate postmodern theology must explicate a doctrine of God as the God of all creation and a doctrine of God as the God of the oppressed. The former doctrine is required to connect theology with reality as such, and the latter doctrine is required for connecting theology to the modern reality of Middle Passage cargo.

A doctrine of God as God of all creation is developed in a variety of constructive postmodern theology indebted to the metaphysics of Whitehead and Hartshorne. This variety of constructive postmodern theology is frequently called "process theology," and when the emphasis is more Hartshornean than Whiteheadian, it is often called "neoclassical theology." A doctrine of God as God of the oppressed is developed in a variety of liberation theology called "black theology" indebted to James H. Cone and other black churchly sources.

Before synthesizing neoclassical metaphysics and black theology, it is important to answer prior questions: "What is neoclassical metaphysics?" (chapter 3) and "What is black theology?" (chapter 4). Also, readers who are new to the science of metaphysics should read "What is Metaphysics?" (appendix A).

Strictly speaking, metaphysics is scientific study of logically necessary existential truths—truths about existence or reality as such. In addition to strict metaphysics, there is a broader sense of metaphysics. Metaphysics more broadly conceived is scientific study of pragmatically necessary existential truths—truths about human existence as such. Neoclassical metaphysics is mainly, but not exclusively, strict metaphysics.[2]

Hartshorne on "Neoclassical" and "Process"

Neoclassical metaphysics is the metaphysical philosophy and theology developed by Hartshorne and Hartshornean scholars. Hartshorne is instructed by Whitehead. Accordingly, neoclassical metaphysics is commonly taken to be part of Whiteheadian process philosophy. Yet, while clearly among the "philosophers of process,"[3] Hartshorne calls his metaphysical philosophy and theology "neoclassical."

Hartshorne has a positive and a negative reason for calling his contributions to process thought "neoclassical." The positive reason is that joining "neo" with "classical" indicates a revision of classical thinking, especially classical Greek philosophy and the now commonly recognized theology Hartshorne calls "classical theism."[4] In *Omnipotence and Other Theological Mistakes* Hartshorne says classical theism is "too strongly influenced by Greek philosophy as medieval scholars knew that philosophy" (1). Classical Greek and medieval philosophical influences contributed to modern classical theism's theological mistakes, including a mistaken conception of omnipotence. For the sake of explicit contrast with classical theism, Hartshorne calls his version of process theology "neoclassical theism" (OOTM, ix), and his metaphysics is called "neoclassical metaphysics" (LP).

Hartshorne's negative reason for favoring "neoclassical" over "process" is that, unlike the term process, neoclassical does not imply commitment to emphasizing process (becoming, change, flux) without equal attention to relativity (social relations, sharing creativity).

Hartshorne says the term neoclassical is noncommittal with regard to which theme (process or relativity) is more essential to metaphysics. This is an advantage because process and relativity are equally essential metaphysical themes. In "The Development of Process Philosophy," Hartshorne says:

The term "process philosophy"—first used by I do not know whom, perhaps my friend Bernard Loomer—is one way of pointing to a profound change which has come over speculative philosophy or metaphysics in the modern period in Europe and America. I have myself often used the more noncommittal phrase "neoclassical metaphysics" for much the same purpose, since the emphasis upon process or becoming, though essential, is only one feature of this new way of viewing reality. Also characteristic is the emphasis upon relations and relativity. (PT, 47–48)

Hartshorne's "neoclassical" metaphysics places equal emphasis upon process and relativity.[5]

Hartshorne says his interests are "nature, God, and man, in about that order."[6] Accordingly, in the present chapter, there is a section on metaphysical aspects of nature followed by a section on metaphysical aspects of theology.

Creative Process and Social Relations in the Metaphysics of Nature

Whitehead on Creative Process

In *Process and Reality* (1929), Whitehead describes his method:

The true method of discovery is like the flight of an aeroplane. It starts from the ground of particular observation; it makes a flight in the thin air of imaginative generalization; and it again lands for renewed observation rendered acute by rational interpretation. (PR, 5)

Whitehead starts by observing experience. Whitehead finds that every occasion of experience is partly (largely) determined by previous occasions of experience, and partly determined by the experiencing self. Whitehead sees the process of occasions of experience contributing to subsequent occasions of experience as a creative process wherein each present occasion makes its own novel contribution to other future occasions. Then, by imaginative generalization, Whitehead hypothesizes that all reality consists of actual occasions experiencing inheritances from the past in partly self-chosen (self-creative) ways, thereby making somewhat novel-creative contributions to future occasions of experience. In each actual occasion of experience, "The many become one, and are increased by one" (PR, 21). Whitehead holds that "creativity" is an ultimate category—"the universal of universals" (PR, 1)—applicable to every actual occasion in some measure, however slight. Although Whitehead's own designation for his philsophy was "philosophy of organism" (PR, 18), his philosophy came to be called "process" because it emphasized the necessarily creative "process of becoming" (PR, 24, 29).

Relative to "process," Whitehead's designation has the advantage of more nearly explicating a metaphysical connection between reality and experience. Individual organisms are experiencing entities. They feel and interact with others. They are social beings in the creative process of contributing to other becomings. Thus, an organic conception of reality denies the mechanical view of nature as mostly bits and particles of inert matter.

Hartshorne on Creative Process and Social Relations

Process and creativity are also ultimates for Hartshorne. In *Creative Synthesis and Philosophic Method* (1970) Hartshorne follows Bergson, Berdyaev, and Whitehead[7] in holding that "creativity" is "a fundamental principle, a category applicable to all reality" (CSPM, 1). He says:

there is a sense in which every individual creates and could not fail to do so while existing at all. *To be is to create.* According to this view, when we praise certain individuals as 'creative,' we can properly mean only that what they create is important or extensive, while what others create is trivial or slight. But what they create cannot be zero, so long as the individuals exist. (CSPM, 1)

Like Whitehead, Hartshorne consults experience (CSPM, 2) and looks for its strictly generic-universal-transcendental features. And like Whitehead, Hartshorne finds that every actual moment of experience is a becoming (process), a "creative synthesis" of determinations by others and self, and that each such moment of becoming contributes to the partial determinations of subsequent others (including one's own future selves). Hartshorne says the process of becoming which characterizes all reality has a "creative-synthetic nature" (CSPM, 15).

Creativity is always shared, argues Hartshorne in "A Philosophy of Shared Creative Experience" (CSPM, chapter 1). The sharing of creativity is a necessary feature of all experience. Sharing of creativity applies to divine experience, human experience, and all other experiences.[8] Concerning universal sharing of creativity, Hartshorne says:

> The logical view of the situation is rather that God, being both self-creative and creative of others, produces creatures which likewise, though in radically inferior ways, are self-determining, and also productive of effects beyond themselves. In this fashion the theological view, with its inconsistencies removed, becomes a philosophy of universal creativity. We must not, however, stop with God and man, as self-creative creators; we must go on to conceive the lower animals, and even atoms, as in some slight or trivial way self-determining and creative of others. For if supreme creativity is the divine nature, and and inferior creativity is man's nature, then the lower animals must be still lower levels of creativity. The effect must in some way express the nature of its cause. How can an infinitely creative being produce an absolutely non-creative being? That which is absolutely devoid of what God supremely possesses— what can it be but the zero of actual existence? (CSPM, 11)

"Sharing of creativity," Hartshorne says, is the "social character of experience" (CSPM, 8).

Hartshorne emphasizes the social and processive character of all reality in *Reality as Social Process* (1953), especially in his chapter on "The Social Conception of the Universe." Hartshorne's method of showing the need to conceive of all things as social includes displaying social aspects of existence for higher animals, many-celled animals without brains, and smaller parts of nature, including even atomic and sub-atomic parts (RSP, 34–37). Throughout the whole of reality from all-inclusive to subatomic, Hartshorne argues, social relations and shared creative-synthetic processes necessarily apply.

Hartshorne on Psychicalism (Panpsychism)

"Psychicalism" is Hartshorne's label for the Whiteheadian doctrine that all actual individuals experience, feel, and respond creatively, exercising some slight or great measure of freedom to be partly creative of self and some subsequent others.[9] Feeling is a "psychical" or psychological term with meaning derived from our human experiences. Starting with human feeling, then *"by analogical extension"* (italics added, CSPM, 155),[10] we can conceive that, in degree and quality, a vastly greater measure of feeling applies to God, and that a much lesser measure applies to single cell organisms, and that still smaller measures of feeling apply to molecules, atoms, and subatomic particles. Although the measures are extremely various, ranging from all-inclusive to subatomic, for every actual individual, experience, feeling, and freedom to respond creatively are never at absolute zero. Physics agrees, Hartshorne says, that "even atoms have bits of freedom" (ZF, 162), and that "the vibratory theory of matter banished merely inert units from science" (1976, 67). Psychicalism holds that experience, feeling, sentience, and other psychical-psychological concepts [knowledge, will, memory, love] are "applicable to all individuals whatever, from atoms to deity" (CSPM, 154).

Because Hartshorne applies experience, feeling, and other psychical concepts to all individuals, he sometimes refers to his psychicalism as "panpsychism." The "pan" in panpsychism comes from Greek meaning "all," as in "panacea" meaning "cure all." "Panpsychism" (meaning "all" individuals are "psychical") emphasizes the universality of psychicalism. Panpsychism or universal psychicalism contradicts the classical dualist distinction between mind and matter, that is, between psychical mind and nonpsychical matter, matter that is purely inert, dead, and wholly uncreative stuff with zero feeling and zero freedom.[11]

Hartshorne's Zero Fallacy

No observation can falsify psychicalism. With respect to actual individuals, zero experience, zero feeling, zero mind or sentience, zero power, zero freedom, or zero creativity are not possible observations. To think such observations are possible is to commit "the zero fallacy." The zero fallacy is the fallacy of thinking it is possible to observe the zero of nonquantum properties. In *Zero Fallacy and Other Essays in Neoclassical Philosophy* (1997), Hartshorne formulates the zero fallacy:

It is time to state the zero fallacy, which should be formulated in logic texts, but is not: with properties of which there can be varying degrees, the zero degree, or total absence, is knowable empirically only if there is a known least quantum or finite minimum, of the property. Planck's constant is an example: it excludes complete continuity in changes by setting an absolute finite minimum. Thus light intensity may be reduced to one photon; less than that is simply no light. I hold that metaphysicians should have anticipated this. Absolute continuity of change, nature "making no leaps," never was or could be an observed fact. . . . A zero of elephants is observable because there is a finite minimum of what can properly be called an elephant. (ZF, 166)

Elsewhere, concerning the zero fallacy, Hartshorne says:

To the standard fallacies of the textbooks, I add the "zero fallacy." "Zero elephants in the immediate vicinity" can be a safe assertion. In contrast, "zero life
or mind" (other than one's own) is unobservable. Such an observation would
have to exclude God, by definition ubiquitous, also deal with the pervasiveness
of microorganisms, and in addition take into consideration that molecules and
atoms are organized wholes, acting as one, and insofar like animals. (DL, 31–32)

Of course rocks, tables, and other inanimate objects do not feel. However, according to Hartshorne, this does not witness against psychicalism because rocks and tables are not individuals. Instead, they are nonindividual collectives—collections of microscopic and subatomic
individuals that do feel.[12] With regard to the impossibility of observing
zero feeling in actual individuals, Hartshorne says:

Of course tables do not feel; but it does not follow that there is no feeling in
them. There is feeling in a flock of birds or in a swarm of bees, but the flock or
the swarm feels nothing. So there can be feeling in a swarm of molecules,
though the swarm does not feel. (CSPM, 142)

A table is a swarm or collection of molecules and atoms. Although the
swarm or collective does not feel, this is not true of its individual parts.
Psychicalism holds that "all individuals (other than mere collectives)
are sentient" (CSPM, 143). And since, with regard to actual individuals, there can be no observational falsification of psychicalism (no
observation of zero feeling, mind, freedom or creativity), for
Hartshorne, psychicalism has metaphysical status.[13]

Creative Process and Social Relations
in the Metaphysics of God

Hartshorne on Divine Relativity (Surrelativism) and Panentheism

In doing theology, Hartshorne's method is "to apply logical analysis to
the religious idea of God" (DR, ix).[14] Religion sees God as creative and
personal, and a "personal God," says Hartshorne, "is one who has
social relations" (DR, x). Hartshorne emphasizes divine social relations
in *The Divine Relativity: A Social Conception of God* (1948).

Nondivine individuals have social-interactive relations with a few
local individuals (and God) for a short while. God, being the unique all-
inclusive individual, has social relations with all individuals forever.

Because the divine relativity is uniquely universal, Hartshorne describes God as "surrelative," meaning supremely relative.[15]

Surrelativism is also called "panentheism" (DR, ix). Hartshorne says that "surrelativism and panentheism are logically the same doctrine with only a difference of emphasis" (DR, 90). Surrelativism emphasizes the superiority and unsurpassability of the divine relativity, while panentheism emphasizes the universal scope of the divine relativity.

Panentheism differs from pantheism. Notice the *"en"* between "pan" and "theism" in "pan*en*theism." According to pantheism, all things together equal God (pan = theos). According to pan-en-theism, all things are in God (pan in theos) and God is more than (transcends) the sum of included things. As a living human person is more than the sum of her/his included cellular parts (as distinct from a human corpse being merely equal to the sum of its cellular parts), so, according to panentheism, God is more than the sum of God's included parts. Unlike pantheism, Hartshornean panentheism explicitly affirms the religious conviction that God is a living, socially interactive, personal individual.[16]

Hartshorne on Divine Relativity Including Absolutes

Logically, there can be nothing to which the all-inclusive one is unrelated. All-inclusiveness entails universal relativity. Since the all-inclusive one includes relations to all included contingent things, "there are contingent properties in God" (DR, 117). Hartshorne says:

> This last is of course the solution accepted by surrelativism. It is the only way to combine, without contradiction, the assertions: God knows all truth, and, not all truths are necessary. (DR, 117)

All-inclusive knowledge includes contingency. Moreover, Hartshorne holds that the divine relativity includes the divine absolutes.

That the concrete "divine relativity" includes and exceeds the abstract "divine absolutes" is Hartshorne's main thesis in *The Divine Relativity*. In the preface, Hartshorne says:

> The main thesis, called Surrelativism, also Panentheism, is that the "relative" or changeable, that which depends upon and varies with varying relationships, includes within itself and in value exceeds the nonrelative, immutable, independent, or "absolute," as the concrete includes and exceeds the abstract. (DR, ix) '

By affirming the divine relativity, neoclassical theism also affirms the necessarily included and exceeded divine absolutes.[17]

Unlike neoclassical theism, classical theism affirms divine absolutes while denying divine relativity. On the one hand, the classical doctrine of a wholly absolute God is rightly motivated by desire to conceive of God as unsurpassably great. On the other hand, this classical doctrine is wrongly instructed by a logical failure to see that the relative includes and exceeds the absolute. Since logic shows that the relative includes and exceeds the nonrelative or absolute, Hartshorne concludes, there is "nothing higher than relative being" (DR, x). Thus, the classical desire to conceive of God as unsurpassably great is better served by the neoclassical affirmation of divine relativity.[18]

Hartshorne's Principle of Dual Transcendence

Hartshorne's neoclassical theology is governed by his "principle of dual transcendence" (OOTM, 44). In contrast with dual transcendence, classical theism offers a half-truth—a single transcendence. In *Omnipotence and Other Theological Mistakes* (1984), Hartshorne identifies "Six Common Mistakes About God" (chapter 1) which, taken together, describe classical theism. Classical theism is characterized by mistaken conceptions of (1) divine perfection, (2) divine omnipotence, (3) divine omniscience, and (4) divine sympathy, plus mistakes about (5) human immortality and (6) human reception of divine revelation.

(1) The classical conception of divine perfection is maximally anti-social in holding a perfect God must be wholly immutable and non-relative in every respect. For neoclassical theism, God is the surrelative "subject of all change" (MVG, 251). Whereas classical theism affirms divine immutability and denies divine change, neoclassical theism affirms both, with change including immutable aspects.

(2) The classical conception of divine omnipotence errs in holding that God is wholly determinative of all actual events. Such talk is non-sense, void of coherent meaning. Neoclassical metaphysics holds that nothing is wholly determinative of anything else. For neoclassical theology, omnipotence means God is partly determinative of all actual events, and partly determined by all actual events; where, by contrast, less powerful entities are partly determinative of some actual events, and partly determined by some actual events.

(3) The classical conception of divine omniscience wrongly holds that whatever happens must have been eternally known as wholly

predetermined in every respect by God. Neoclassical theology holds that omniscience means all-knowing, and knowing all things as they really are means knowing the actually determined as actually determined and knowing the not yet fully determined (not yet actual) as not yet fully determined. Classical talk of knowing the partly indeterminate as already wholly determined is logical nonsense.

(4) The classical conception of divine goodness wrongly holds that God is impassible or unsympathetic, an "unmoved mover" (Aristotle) who does not suffer. Rather than conceiving of God as an unmoved mover, neoclassical theology conceives of God as unsurpassably moved (and unsurpassably moving). Neoclassical theology holds that divine goodness includes supreme and unsurpassable sympathy. The all-inclusive one experiences every experience, suffering every pain and joy fully.

(5) Classical theism frequently errs in conceiving of human immortality as "a career after death" (OOTM, 4).[19] Instead of the classical view of "subjective immortality" as a never-ending, after-death career, Hartshorne holds to a Whiteheadian doctrine of "objective immortality" according to which "an entire career, with all its concrete values, is an imperishable possession of deity" (OOTM, 40).[20]

(6) Classical theism is marked by an erroneous conception of infallible special revelation (OOTM, 5). Logically, divinely inspired humans cannot produce wholly infallible documents or doctrines because any synthesis of the wholly infallible and the partly fallible must yield a partly fallible product.

By emphasizing necessary divine absolutes and denying or ignoring divine relativity, the single transcendence of classical theism produces a supremely anti-social (nonrelative) conception of God—God as a wholly other, immutable, unmoved mover. By contrast, the dual transcendence of neoclassical theism yields a supremely social-relational conception of God. Hartshorne says, "Maximizing relativity as well as absoluteness in God [dual transcendence] enables us to conceive him as a supreme person" (DR, 142). Logical metaphysical analysis confirms the religious idea of God as the supremely relative person.

Ogden on God as Supremely Relative

In agreement with Hartshorne's neoclassical view of God, Schubert M. Ogden says the "the supremely relative one" of Christian scripture is "far from being the God of classical philosophy, who is in no way related to others" (EA, 17). According to Ogden, God is unique because God interacts with all others, while nondivine individuals interact with only some others (and God). Ogden says, "whereas any individual other than God interacts with some others only, God interacts with all, not only acting on them but also being acted on by them" (1985, 96). God is eternally and universally interactive. God is the one to whom all things make partial differences, and the one who makes partial differences to all things (here again is dual transcendence). In contrast to God, we are ones to whom some things make partial differences, and ones who make partial differences to some things.[21] As with Hartshorne's logical analysis of the religious idea of God, according to Ogden's specifically Christian analysis, God is supremely relative.

God of All Creation

In its account of both nature and God, neoclassical metaphysics emphasizes the strict metaphysical necessity of creative processes and social relations. God is supremely creative and supremely social, sharing creativity with all creation. God is universally and eternally interactive. God is comprehensive. Nothing is external to God. Nothing is unrelated to God. God is omnipresent, all-powerful, all-embracing, all-experiencing, all-knowing, and all-loving. God is the God of all creation. Distinct from all others, God is the all-inclusive one to whom all things make partly determinative differences and who makes partly determinative and wholly righteous differences to all things.

4

What is Black Theology?

James H. Cone

The first book explicitly calling itself a "Black Theology" is James H. Cone's *Black Theology and Black Power* (1969). Here Cone conceives of "Black Theology" as a black Christian theological appropriation of the philosophy of "Black Power."

Black power is a radical and explicitly separatist political philosophy that was formulated in the context of black struggles for liberty during the late 1960s. Two of the earliest formulations of the philosophy of black power are: *Black Power: The Politics of Liberation in America* (1967) by Stokely Carmichael (Kwame Turé) and Charles V. Hamilton; and "Black Power" (chapter 2) in *Where Do We Go From Here: Chaos or Community?* (1967) by Martin Luther King Jr.[1] Also, "black nationalism," which calls for a separate black nation carved from U.S. territories, is a closely related black separatist philosophy developed in Floyd McKissick's *Three Fifths of a Man* (1969). The philosophy of black power calls for a separate black political party and other independent, self-directed black liberation efforts.

In *Black Theology and Black Power*, Cone identifies contribution to the black struggle for freedom as the criterion for identifying the gospel of Jesus Christ. Cone writes:

Black Theology must say: 'If the doctrine is compatible with or enhances the drive for black freedom, then it is the gospel of Jesus Christ. If the doctrine is against or indifferent to the essence of blackness as expressed in Black Power, then it is the work of the Antichrist.' It is as simple as that. (BTBP, 121)

Cone sees the gospel of Jesus Christ as a liberating gospel and black power as that gospel's contemporary expression.

In his second book, *A Black Theology of Liberation* (1970), Cone defines black theology as a Christian theology, and Christian theology as liberation theology. Here Cone says:

Christian theology is a theology of liberation. It is *a rational study of the being of God in the world in the light of the existential situation of an oppressed community, relating the forces of liberation to the essence of the gospel, which is Jesus Christ.* (BTL, 17)

Like other Christian liberation theologies, black liberation theology identifies God as "God of the oppressed." In his book *God of the Oppressed* (1975), Cone maintains that God sides with the poor and oppressed in their struggles for liberty. According to Cone, black theology is a Christian theology of liberation, a study of biblical and churchly praxis and logos about theos showing what the gospel of Jesus Christ contributes to the contemporary liberation struggles of poor and oppressed communities.

For Cone, the God of the oppressed is the God of all creation. This idea is deeply rooted in African-American Christianity. For example, this idea was precisely expressed by Frederick Douglass (1817–1895), an African Methodist Episcopal Zion clergyman and abolitionist (Walls, 150). Douglass argued that, even though slaveholders seldom recognized it, the abolition of slavery was really in their best interests. In some important ways, even slaveholders were oppressed by slavery, and therefore, ultimately, the struggle for liberty favored everyone. Accordingly, Douglass identified "the Most High, who is ever *the God of the oppressed*" (italics added) as the God of all creation—"our common Father and Creator" (MBMF, 421–28).

Churchly Origins

Cone's theological appropriation of black power was preceded by black churchly affirmations of black power. The most famous of such affirmations was the "Black Power Statement" signed by forty-eight of North America's most prominent black clergy and published as a full page ad in *The New York Times* on 31 July 1966. Cone distinguishes black theology from other theologies by pointing to these and other black churchly origins. Unlike many other theologies, black theology was not born in seminaries and universities. Instead, black theology originated from black churchly liberation struggles.[2]

Black churchly affirmations of black separatist thinking (black power) are consistent with early black church history. In North America, independent black churches and denominations have black separatist origins.

For instance, consider the black separatist origin of the African Methodist Episcopal Church. In 1787, white members of St. George Methodist Episcopal Church in Philadelphia were so oppressive of their black members that Richard Allen (a former slave), Absalom Jones, and other black members separated themselves from that white congregation and formed their own independent black congregation called the Free African Society.[3] This growing Allenite congregation built and dedicated Bethel Church in Philadelphia in 1794 (AMEZ, 28). Then in April 1816, the Mother Bethel congregation united with black separatist Methodists from Baltimore and other places to create the African Methodist Episcopal Church (BRBR, 80–84).

The African Methodist Episcopal Zion Church also has a black separatist origin. In 1796, white members of the John Street Methodist Episcopal Church of New York City were so oppressive of their black members that James Varick, Peter Williams (a former slave), and other black members separated themselves from that white congregation and formed a separate black Methodist society. By 1800, that society had become Zion Church. In 1801, Zion Church was incorporated as the African Methodist Episcopal Church in New York City. In 1820, this now larger congregation of Zionites calling itself the African Methodist Episcopal Zion Church of New York City united with Asbury African Methodist Episcopal Church of New York City and officially "voted themselves out of the Methodist Episcopal Church" (AMEZ, 48), thereby creating the "African Methodist Episcopal Church in America" (AMEZ, 49; BRBR, 85). According to the Founders' Address, the differences leading to separation were ethical and practical—matters of "ecclesiastical government" and "limited access" to ordination and other churchly privileges "in consequence of the difference of color" (AMEZ, 49). At an 1848 General Conference, the African Methodist Episcopal Church in America distinguished itself from the Philadelphia Allenites (also called African Methodist Episcopal Church) and reaffirmed its Zionite origin by changing its name to the "African Methodist Episcopal Zion Church" (AMEZ, 50; BC, 57–58).

Many African-American congregations, churches, and denominations share a similarly separatist heritage. Protestant churches were the home of North America's earliest experiment with black-white racial integration. Unfortunately, within early American churches, white-black relations were relentlessly unequal and oppressive. As a result, whenever black Christians secured enough liberty to do so, they exchanged oppressive integration for liberating separatism. By the end of the U.S. Civil War, African-American Christians were completing a mass exodus from Euro-American churches.[4] In the areas of religion and church, early American black religion was doing what a contemporary philosophy of black power prescribes for politics and other areas—pursuing a liberating separatism.[5] Gayraud S. Wilmore's *Black Religion and Black Radicalism: An Interpretation of the Religious History of Afro-American People* (1973) shows that throughout its history in North America, black religion has been a relentless source of black radicalism. Accordingly, the black churchly embrace of radical separatist black power yielding black theology should have been no surprise.

Generic Conceptions

In addition to the originating conceptions of black theology as a black churchly appropriation of the philosophy of black power and a black Christian theology of liberation, there are also more general or generic conceptions of black theology. A generic black theology need not explicitly embrace black power. And generic black theology admits black theological deliberations from non-Christian religions, especially from traditional African non-Christian religions. Generically conceived, black theology is the critical and constructive study of logos about theos and liberation explicitly rooted in black experiences.

As permitted by a more generic conception of black theology, not all black theologies are Christian, and not all are theistic. But virtually all black theologies seek to be liberating.

For example, in *Is God A White Racist? A Preamble to Black Theology* (1973), William R. Jones embraces nontheistic "black humanism" (xxi) and prescribes that theistic black liberation theologies embrace a "humanocentric theism"—a "hybrid of humanism and theism" (186–88). By emphasizing human responsibility Jones seeks to liberate black theology from doctrines of divine determination which discourage human struggles for self-determination. Black humanism is also embraced in *Why Lord? Suffering and Evil in Black Theology* (1995), in which Anthony B. Pinn offers a critical examination of African-American responses to slavery, suffering, and other evils. Pinn rejects "suffering servant" motifs because they discourage liberation struggles, and he advocates a black humanism that "denies the existence of God and holds humans fully accountable for the existence and removal of moral evil in the world" (WL, 10–11). Here black logos about theos and liberation requires denying classical theos and classical omnipotence for the sake of encouraging liberation struggles.[6]

Womanist Theology

Womanist theology is logos about theos, survival, and liberation, constructed by black women.[7] Alice Walker's development of the "womanist" concept in *In Search of Our Mothers' Gardens: Womanist Prose* (1983) is an originating reference for womanist thought. Black womanist theologians indebted to Walker find that, like mainstream Protestant and Catholic traditions, black separatist Christianity exhibits an unrighteous patriarchal bias that is oppressive of woman and children, and oppressive of all erotic experiences outside monogamous male-female marriage.[8]

Black female theologians following Alice Walker in identifying themselves as "womanist" agree that oppressive patriarchal theology and the oppression of woman and children are unrighteous, but not all embrace her call for being less restrictive of erotic possibilities. For example, Cheryl J. Sanders is a womanist theologian who is critical of some of the erotic-sexual liberties embraced by Walker's definition of womanist.[9] Womanist theologians subtract or add content according to their own critical and constructive deliberations. Some womanist theologies are specifically Christian, some are not. All affirm black women's right and responsibility to name black women's experiences, and to employ those experiences as criteria for meaning and truth.[10]

Womanist theologies characteristically offer conceptions of God liberated from traditional patriarchal images. For instance, Alice Walker's conception of God is emphasized by Cheryl Townsend Gilkes in "'A Conscious Connection to All That Is': The Color Purple as Subversive and Critical Ethnography" (ES, 275–96). Gilkes notes that Shug (a character in Walker's novel *The Color Purple* [1982]) argues that God is not an old white patriarch. Instead, "God is everything. . . . Everything that is or ever was or ever will be" (CP, 190; CP 1985 edition, 202–03). Gilkes quotes Walker as saying:

No one is exempt from the possibility of a conscious connection to All That Is [God]. Not the poor. Not the suffering. Not the writer sitting in the open field. (ES, 275; CP 1992 edition, xi)

And Gilkes notes that another character, Nettie, discovers this nonpatri-archical understanding of God is liberating. Gilkes and other womanist theologians evaluate logos about theos by reference to survival and lib-eration. The most liberating conceptions of God are valued over others.

Womanist theology has improved upon black theology's emphasis upon race, Latin American liberation theology's emphasis upon class, and feminist theology's empasis upon gender. Womanist theology emphasizes liberation from race, class, and gender-based oppres-sions.[11] Furthermore, womanist theology encourages concern for the well-being of nonhuman creatures and creations.[12]

Womanist theology agrees with neoclassical antidualism. Classical dualism separates the physical from the spiritual, and it values disem-bodied spirituality over embodied existence. Most womanist theolo-gians reject classical dualism. In *Sisters of Dust, Sisters of Spirit* (1998) Karen Baker-Fletcher holds that "humans are both earthy and spiri-tual," that Jesus "was born of dust and spirit" (7), and that God is "fully embodied in creation" (18). Similarly, Evelyn L. Parker describes Christian spirituality as "a wedding of the physical with the spiritual" (TD, viii). Womanist influence encourages black theology to abandon classical dualism.

God of the Oppressed

Black theology insists that the God of all creation is also the liberating God of the oppressed. That God is the God of all creation is "good news" to all creation. That the God of all creation is also the God of the oppressed is "good news" to all creation *and* "good news to the oppressed" and "to the poor" (Isaiah 61:1, Luke 4:18). Black theology favors the more inclusive doctrine because the less inclusive doctrine is not adequate to the needs of enslaved, impoverished, and otherwise oppressed populations.

Part III

Neoclassical Metaphysics
and Black Theology:
A Black Atlantic Synthesis

5

Toward a Metaphysics of Struggle

Given that strict metaphysical truths are indifferent to all contingencies, by definition, for overcoming that contingency called modernity, metaphysical inquiry is inadequate. But inadequate does not mean inessential or unimportant. Strict metaphysical truths are affirmed, at least implicitly, by any factual claim (true or false). Moreover, explicating metaphysical truth is an important contribution to correcting many modern philosophical, theological, and ethical errors.

Here in part three, neoclassical metaphysics and black theology are brought together. Black theology introduces concern with contingent social relations, including especially divine and human relations to oppression, liberation struggles, and mothership connections. This synthesis of neoclassical metaphysics and black theology yields a black Atlantic account of strictly and broadly metaphysical aspects of struggle (chapter 5), power (chapter 6), and ethical deliberation (chapter 7).

Struggle for Freedom as Inevitable

"The struggle continues" is a popular saying among black freedom fighters in southern Africa and elsewhere. And struggle for freedom or liberation struggle is a prominent theme in African-American history. Vincent Harding says struggle for freedom and justice is "the central theme of black history in the United States" (TR, xx). This chapter is about the metaphysical aspects of struggle, especially struggle for freedom.[1]

Harding's *There is a River: The Black Struggle for Freedom in America* (1981) is a historical survey of the African-American struggle for freedom. Beginning with captivity in Africa, moving "from the shores of Africa" (the title of chapter 1) across the Atlantic as cargo on slave ships, and extending through generations to the end of North American slavery in 1865, Harding sees a continuous struggle for freedom. In describing a slave ship captain's effort to end the struggle of enslaved captives by making an example of a rebellious captive, killing him, and hoisting his body high up on a ship's mast, Harding says, "Snelgrave probably did not know it then, but even if he had hoisted the insurrectionary up into the clouds, the struggle would not have ended" (TR, 11). Harding describes African and African-American struggle for freedom as inevitable.

Emphatically, four times, at the start of four paragraphs in the first chapter, Harding says, "Struggle was inevitable" (TR, 3, 5, 10, 22). In emphasizing the inevitability of black struggle for freedom, Harding is not merely describing actual past struggles. Rather than saying merely "Struggle occurred," which is precisely what the empirical historical data supports, Harding says more—that "Struggle was inevitable." For Harding, struggle for freedom is an inevitable human response to oppression.

Harding employs the "metaphor of the river" (TR, xix) to describe the history of black struggle for freedom. Harding's use of the river metaphor resembles the Whiteheadian-Hartshornean emphasis upon process and creativity. Harding describes the "river of black struggle" as a fluid-flowing and transforming movement continuously created by people and continuously creative of people. Harding says:

> we are indeed the river, and at the same time . . . the river is more than us—generations more, millions more. . . . [T]he river of black struggle is people, but it is also the hope, the movement, the transformative power that humans create and that creates them, us, and makes them, us, new persons. So we black people are the river; the river is us. The river is in us, created by us, flowing out of us, surrounding us, re-creating us and this entire nation. (TR, xix)

The history of this river of struggle is a history of a flowing transformative and creative process.

Creativity is also emphasized in Harding's account of the river's inevitability. Harding describes black liberation struggle as an inevitable response to compressed creativity. In describing the struggle of captives in Africa, Harding says such struggle "was to be expected" because "too much *human creativity*, too much human hope *was compressed* in those castles and dungeons for the struggle to be denied" (TR, 9; italics added). Captivity, slavery, and oppression compress creativity. According to Harding's anthropology, naturally creative humans inevitably struggle against compression of creativity.

Given seriously oppressive compression of human creativity, struggle for liberty is certain. More than once I heard black power advocate Kwame Turé proclaim in public speech with great emphasis, "Until there is liberty, there will be struggle and struggle and struggle and struggle!"[2] Turé was describing, predicting, prescribing, and promising black liberation struggle.

Though liberation struggle is an inevitable response to oppression, the nature of that struggle and the meaning of liberty are highly variable. Harding reports that while captives on a slave ship were still within sight of the African coast, the struggle was "to remain in our homeland" (TR, 9), and often this meant escaping the shackles, diving into the water, and swimming back to the African coast. Later, when the slave ship was far out into the Atlantic, frequently the "the only possible struggle for most captives was to stay alive," to survive (TR, 15). And generations later, slaves born on the American continents faced different circumstances requiring different struggles for different liberties. Harding shows that "from place to place, time to time, and setting to setting, the nature of our struggle was to be transformed and the questions reshaped" (TR, 15). Harding holds that because of changing circumstances, the precise "definition of the struggle for freedom" is "fluid" (TR, 26).[3]

Did struggle occur? Of course it did. "Struggle was inevitable." We can know this from general anthropology plus a little history. The more difficult and interesting questions are about the variable, contingent aspects of struggle. What kinds of struggle occurred? How more or less successful were the various kinds of struggle? What do past failures and successes imply for present and future struggles?[4] For Harding, understanding both the variable and constant aspects of actual historical struggles is essential to understanding the river and to guiding "its continuing movement toward freedom" (TR, 23).

According to Harding's analysis, where there is serious oppression (serious compression of creativity), struggle for freedom is an inevitable human response. This truth is not mere historical description of what actually happened once upon a time. This truth is a general principle of human existence.

Karen Baker-Fletcher's *A Singing Something: Womanist Reflections on Anna Julia Cooper* (1994) offers a theological explanation for the inevitability of liberation struggle. Baker-Fletcher finds Anna Julia Cooper (1859–1964) "describing God as a 'Singing Something' that rises up within humanity in every nation to cry out against injustice" (SS, 16). Where there is injustice/oppression, the omnipresent influence of the divine singing something inspires human liberation struggle.

Black theology holds liberation struggle is divinely inspired. According to J. Deotis Roberts's "The Holy Spirit and Liberation: A Black Perspective," liberation struggle is one of the "fruits of the Spirit."[5] Similarly, in *God of the Oppressed* Cone speaks of God as a spirit "that guides and moves the people in their struggle" (21). Where oppression is experienced, the Holy Spirit inspires liberation struggle. Again, now with explicit theological and pneumatological explanations, the inevitability of struggle against oppression is a general principle of human existence.

Even more generally, Howard Thurman (1900–1981) holds that struggle against oppression is characteristic of all oppressed creaturely life, not just human life. I was present during Thurman's Spring 1978 visit to Hood Theological Seminary at Livingstone College in Salisbury, North Carolina, when he recalled that on one occasion during his childhood in Daytona Beach, he happened upon a tiny green snake crawling along a dirt path. In a mischievous way typical of a child, Thurman pressed his bare foot on top of the little snake. Immediately, the snake began to struggle against this oppression. Young Thurman felt the tremor of the snake's struggle vibrate up his leg and through his body. Generalizing from this experience, Thurman concluded that struggle against oppression is natural for all God's creatures, including little green snakes.[6]

Liberation Struggle as Conditional Necessity

Conceiving of liberation struggle as an inevitable response to oppression does not require that liberation struggle be conceived as strictly necessary. Struggle against oppression (liberation struggle) is not a strict necessity because oppression is an unnecessary, conditional, and extreme circumstance. In *Love and Conflict: A Covenantal Model of Christian Ethics* (1984), Joseph L. Allen prescribes "covenant love" as "the basic moral standard of Christian ethics" (9) and the priority of "the inclusive covenant" (152). Allen holds that struggle derives from conflict, and that both conflict and harmony are inescapable. Allen says conflict is "an inescapable feature of life" and that conflict is "never separable from some degree of harmony" (LC, 9).

The inescapability of conflict does not necessitate oppression. To the contrary, Allen holds that a "fundamental harmony is compatible with certain kinds of conflict, and that is what we must seek" (LC, 98). Allen joins liberationist thinking in conceiving of oppression as an extreme, serious, and unnecessary manifestation of conflict. According to Allen's reading of liberation theology, "the idea of oppression" communicates extremely serious blameworthy deprivations and exploitations (LC, 171). Allen says:

> Liberation theologians specifically identify the problem they have experienced as oppression, and not simply misfortune or human error. The destitution of masses of people, the great disproportion between their power and that of the privileged, and the way social structures perpetuate these problems—these things have come about through people's exploiting other people. Misfortune is lamentable, error may or may not be our own responsibility, but oppression is especially blameworthy. To label the matter oppression is to communicate the seriousness and the responsibility that are appropriate to the situation. (LC, 171)

Throughout the literature of oppression and liberation, "oppression" describes a serious and unnecessary extreme such as slavery, and "liberation struggle" describes an inevitable response to suffering from oppression.

Logically, any response to any contingency is a contingent response. And even an inevitable response, such as liberation struggle, to a contingent-conditional circumstance, such as oppression, is not a strict necessity. Though not a strict necessity, an inevitable response can be described as a conditional necessity. "Conditional necessity" is called "hypothetical necessity" by Eugene H. Peters.

According to Peters's analysis of Hartshorne's method,[7] "hypothetical necessities" and "metaphysical necessities" are different "species of nonfactual truth" (EA, 3). For Hartshorne, says Peters, hypothetical necessities are about relations between contingent entities. Given the actualization of said contingent entities and relations, certain consequences necessarily obtain. However, hypothetical necessites, says Peters, "neither affirm nor deny the actuality of those entities to which they attribute the analytic connections" (EA, 3).

The doctrine of inevitable liberation struggle says if the hypothesis "there is oppression" is true, inevitably, those suffering from oppression will respond with struggle for freedom/liberty. Whether or not oppression is actually present is a contingent matter, not a matter of strict metaphysical necessity. If oppression were strictly necessary, there could be no possiblity of overcoming it. Yet, throughout the literature of oppression and liberation struggle, there is hope and expectation that "we shall overcome" oppression.

Womanist Hope and Expectation

Womanist literature affirms inevitable struggle for freedom and a hope which expects progress in the struggle to overcome oppression. The black womanist essays in *Embracing the Spirit: Womanist Perspectives on Hope, Salvation and Transformation* (1997) include witnesses affirming both inevitable struggle and hope for liberation. For instance, Alice Walker's view that oppressed people "don't never get used to it" is emphasized by Cheryl Townsend Gilkes,[8] who says:

No matter the limited comfort zones that are carved out of segments of personal experience; people, Walker points out, are never really comfortable with suffering. The fact that people "don't never get used to it" is a catalyst for activism. . . . (ES, 292)

According to Gilkes and Walker, liberation struggle is inevitable because people never get used to being oppressed.

Expectation of liberation is evident in Mary M. Townes's contribution to *Embracing the Spirit,* in which she defines hope as including desire and expectation.[9] She says:

To desire but not to expect is not hope, for though you may desire the moon, you hardly hope for it. To expect but not to desire is not hope, for who that expects his or her loved one to die could be said to hope for it? But to desire, and to expect the desire's fulfillment, that is hope. And we are saved by hope. (ES, 4)

Townes and other contributors to *Embracing the Spirit* agree that womanist hope includes expectation of liberation.[10]

In *Trouble Don't Last Always: Emancipatory Hope Among African American Adolescents* (2003) by Evelyn L. Parker, hope and expectation of liberty are rooted in consciousness of our inheritances from the past, consciousness of capacity to be partly determinative of the future ("agency"), and consciousness of relations to God. Parker finds that without these roots, many adolescents lapse into hopelessness. Parker defines emancipatory hope as "expectation that dominant powers of racism, classism, sexism, and heterosexism will be toppled and that African American adolescents have agency in God's vision for dismantling these powers of domination" (TD, viii). Such expectful hope is grounded in reality. Liberation struggle is not futile because oppression is unnecessary and subject to being overcome.

God of the Oppressed as Conditional Necessity

Peters's analysis of Hartshorne reveals a distinction between two kinds of necessary truths: metaphysical necessities and hypothetical necessities. Although Peters's Hartshornean category of hypothetical necessity is about relations between contingent entities, hypothetical necessity can be extended to apply to relations between humans and God. Accordingly, the idea that God is "God of the oppressed" can be described as a hypothetical or conditional necessity.

The conception of God as "God of the oppressed" is about how the God of all creation responds to oppression. Response to oppression is not strictly necessary because oppression is unnecessary. However, given actual oppression, according to black theology, the inevitable divine response is to sing something inspiring liberation struggle (Baker-Fletcher), and to be the liberating God of the oppressed (Cone). This inevitable response is a conditional necessity.

Our knowledge of this conditional necessity is partly derived from analyzing human experiences. According to black Atlantic analyses, the experiences of suffering from oppression inevitably result in desire for liberty and liberation struggle. And insofar as God experiences these experiences, God favors relief from oppression. When the strict metaphysical necessity that "God experiences all experience" is conjoined with conditional-contingent facts about actual experiences of suffering from oppression, this yields a conditional necessity—that the God of all creation is the God of the oppressed.

6

Toward a Metaphysics of Power

Why Analyze Power?

Black Theology

Black theology requires analysis of power. In *Black Theology and Black Power* (1969), Cone conceives of black theology as a black Christian appropriation of black power. Black power philosophies are mainly about the particularities of black power and black-white relations. As developed prior to Cone's book, and in subsequent black empowerment theologies, philosophies of black power have not included much systematic analysis of the most general aspects of power.[1] Critically appropriating an empowerment philosophy requires recourse to a systematic analysis of power. And a fully explicit analysis of power includes both particular and universal, contingent and necessary, factual and metaphysical aspects.[2]

Black Theodicy

Another reason for analyzing power is that theodicy requires such analysis. Theodicy is the problem of reconciling experiences of suffering from evil (including natural evils such as sickness and moral evils such as slavery or other oppression) with theological doctrines affirming that God is omnibenevolent (all-good) and omnipotent (all-powerful). The term "theodicy" derives from the work of Gottfried Wilhelm von Leibniz (1646–1716). Leibniz combined the Greek "theo" for God with the Greek "dike" for righteousness or justice to form "theo-dicy." Leibniz was addressing the problem of reconciling gross moral evils with divine righteousness and divine power.[3] The problem particular to black theology is reconciling black experiences of slavery and oppression with black faith in divine goodness and divine power. Black and other theodicies require an analysis of power.

Absolute and Relational Conceptions of Power

Omnipotence

Omnipotence is sometimes held to mean that God is all-powerful in the sense of being wholly determinative of everyone and everything. When starting with this understanding of omnipotence, there is no way of coherently affirming actual evil without denying omnibenevolence.

Hartshorne views this "classical" understanding of omnipotence (that God is wholly-absolutely determinative of everything) as a theological mistake. In *Omnipotence and Other Theological Mistakes*, Hartshorne prescribes an alternative "neoclassical" conception of omnipotence.

According to the neoclassical correction, omnipotence properly means God is partly determinative of all things and partly determined by all things. The contrast between omnipotence, neoclassically conceived, and lesser potence is the contrast between interacting perfectly with all things and interacting imperfectly with only some things.[4] Hartshorne says all-powerful properly means "that God has the highest conceivable form of power and that this power extends to all things—not as, with us, being confined to a tiny corner of the cosmos" (OOTM, 26).

Ogden conceives of God as having two essential aspects: a "relatively more active aspect" and a "relatively more passive aspect" (1985, 96). The more *active* aspect refers to God acting on God's self and all others. The more *passive* aspect refers to God being acted upon by the divine self and all others. Nondivine individuals have relatively more active and passive aspects as well, but they interact with only some others, not all others. In "The Metaphysics of Faith and Justice," Ogden says the following:

Therefore, even the universal individual called "God" must be conceived as having two essential aspects: a relatively more active aspect in which it acts on or makes a difference to both itself and all others and a relatively more passive aspect in which all others as well as itself act on or make a difference to it. Thus the uniqueness of God in comparison with all other individuals does not lie in God's only acting on others and in no way being acted on by them, but rather in the strictly universal scope of God's field of interaction with others as well as with self. Whereas any other individual interacts with itself for a finite time only, God's acting on Godself and being acted on by Godself has never begun nor will it ever end. And so, too, with respect to interaction with others: whereas any individual other than God interacts with some others only, God interacts with all, not only acting on them but also being acted on by them. (1985, 96)

Ogden holds that God is eternally and universally interactive (making differences to all others and being made different by all others), while all others are, for a relatively short while, locally interactive (making differences to some others and being made different by some others).

For Ogden and Hartshorne, the differences made by and to God, like the differences made by and to all others, are partial determinations or influences, not total-absolute determinations. The classical doctrine of "absolute determinism" is rejected by neoclassical thought. Concerning absolute or unqualified determinism, in *Creative Synthesis and Philosophic Method*, Hartshorne says the following:

Here Peirce, Bergson, and Whitehead are at one. For them as for me determinism, taken without qualification, is categorial confusion or contradiction. (CSPM, 61)

I conclude that determinism is absolutely unverifiable, and therefore affirms no conceivable state of existence. (CSPM, 166)

In principle, determinism in the absolute sense, like so many absolutes, is useless. It does no harm only if it does nothing. Relative determinism, thinking in terms of futuristic outlines of possibility and probability, with boundaries of necessity, is indeed useful. More, it is what we all, determinists or not, unconsciously or not, live by. Nothing else is or could be lived by. The rest, as Peirce said, is make-believe, mere talk. (CSPM, 204)

Determinism is a metaphysical blunder . . . science and common sense require no absolute determinism, only a qualified or relative one. (CSPM, 214)

And in *Omnipotence and Other Theological Mistakes*, Hartshorne says absolute determinism has "no consistent practical meaning" (19), and "laws implying determinism . . . describe no coherently conceivable world" (20–21). Hartshorne holds absolute determinism is confused, self-contradictory, "absolutely unverifiable," "a metaphysical blunder," not required by science or common sense, and mere "useless" talk affirming nothing. Absolute determinism is incoherent, absurd, meaningless nonsense. The only meaningful alternative is "relative determinism."

The contrast between divine determinations and mere creaturely determinations is not the contrast between being wholly determinative (absolute determinism) and being partly determinative (relative determinism). Rather, the contrast is between being partly determinative of *all* things-individuals-events and being partly determinative of only *some* things-individuals-events.

An omnipotent God is partly determinative of *all* things-individuals-events (transmitting partly determinative influences to all) and partly determined by *all* things-individuals-events (receiving partly determinative influences from all). We creatures of lesser potence/power are partly determinative of *some* relatively few things-individuals-events (and God) and partly determined by *some* relatively few things-individuals-events (and God).

Omnipotence is universal and eternal interactivity. Lesser potence is local interactivity for a relatively short time. According to an interactive (active and passive rather than merely active) conception of power, "all-powerful" means interacting with all powers, not being the only power.

Omnipotence and Theodicy

Reconceiving divine power is the key to solving the theodicy problem. As demonstrated by William R. Jones's criticism of black liberation theologies holding to a classical conception of omnipotence, black experiences of suffering from slavery and white racism indicate that a wholly determinative God must be a "white racist" (IGWR). If omnipotence is understood to mean that God is wholly determinative of all events (including the main events of modernity—transatlantic slavery and colonialism), then there is no avoiding the conclusion that God is a white racist. Jones proves that omnibenevolence is unavoidably falsified by combining historical facts about gross moral evil with a classical conception of omnipotence.

However, given a neoclassical conception of omnipotence (universal interactivity, rather than universal absolute determinism), omnipotence can be reconciled with gross moral evil without refuting omnibenevolence.[5] Creaturely experiences are always experiences of interactions with some creaturely others and God, plus the experiencing creature's own novel-creative contributions, never experiences of interaction with God alone. The partly determinative contributions of nondivine selves and nondivine others are fully sufficient to account for all experiences of evil. Hence, evil does not witness against the omnibenevelence of an omnipotent God where omnipotence is neo-classically conceived.

Relational-Interactive Power

According to Hartshorne, the theologically mistaken classical conception of omnipotence is inconsistent with the religious idea of God.[6] Rather than being rooted in religious faith, the classical conception of omnipotence is rooted in classical philosophical errors about power as such.

According to classical philosophy, absolute determination is the greatest conceivable power. Thus, by classical measure, the neoclassical conception of divine power yields a God of lesser power. Hartshorne disagrees. In a section of *Omnipotence and Other Theological Mistakes* called "Two Meanings of 'All-Powerful,'" Hartshorne argues that the classical meaning of all-powerful is "nonsense," and that the neoclassical meaning is "the highest conceivable form of power" (10–26, 38). Hartshorne says the following:

omnipotence as usually conceived is a false or indeed absurd ideal. . . . (OOTM, 17)

As a final verbal clarification, I remark that if by 'all-powerful' we mean that God has the highest conceivable form of power and that this power extends to all things—not as, with us, being confined to a tiny corner of the cosmos—and *if this is what the word 'omnipotent' can be understood to mean, then yes, God is omnipotent.* . . . God has power uniquely excellent in quality and scope, in no respect inferior to any coherently conceivable power. In power, as in all prop-erties, God is exalted beyond legitimate criticism or fault finding. In this power I believe. But it is not power to have totally unfree or "absolutely con-trolled" creatures. For that is nonsense. (OOTM, 26; italics added)

Thus, according to Hartshorne, the neoclassical conception of omnipotence does not make God a lesser power.[7]

Townes's Black Womanist Conception of Power

Unlike the black theologies rooted in classical theism criticized by Jones (IGWR), black womanist thought conceives of power in ways more nearly neoclassical than classical. Black womanist thought faults the traditional classical conception of power for its oppressive patriarchal character.

In *A Troubling in My Soul: Womanist Perspectives on Evil and Suffering* (1993), Emilie M. Townes describes the "traditional concept of power" in terms of requiring submissive obedience to invulnerable authority (86). In place of this traditional authoritarian and patriarchal conception of power, Townes prescribes conceiving of "power as cooperation" and "shared authority" (TMS, 86–87).

For Townes and other black womanists, cooperative or shared power is *not* a lesser form of power. The womanist conception of power is more neoclassical than classical insofar as it joins neoclassical thought against classical thought in refusing to regard shared power as a lesser form of power.

Loomer's "Two Conceptions of Power"

In his essay "Two Conceptions of Power," Bernard Loomer joins Hartshorne in identifying "Two Meanings of 'All-Powerful'" (OOTM, 10). Loomer identifies two conceptions of power as such. There is a *traditional conception of power* as transmitting influences, and a *relational conception of power* as transmitting and receiving influences. The traditional conception is called "linear power." Linear power is about exerting an influence over others that is "unilateral," "one-directional," and "nonmutual in its relationality" (TCP, 8). "Ideally, its aim is to create the largest effect on the other while being minimally influenced by the other" (TCP, 8). For Loomer, linear power is a metaphysically mistaken conception of power. Loomer holds that power is "relational in character" (TCP, 17). For metaphysical and moral reasons, Loomer prescribes replacing "linear power" with "relational power" (TCP, 18).

As with Hartshorne and Townes, for Loomer, relational power is greater than linear power. According to Loomer's relational conception of power, "capacity both to influence others and to be influenced by others" (TCP, 17) is more inclusive than capacity to influence only. Linear power is one-directional. Relational power includes both directions of influence. Hence, relational power is greater.

There is no such thing as wholly determinative influence. Absolute determinism is nonsense. Influence is partly determinative (whether largely determinative or minimally determinative) or nothing. Clearly, capacity to transmit partly determinative influences together with capacity to receive partly determinative influences (relational power) is more inclusive than capacity to transmit only, and more inclusive than the capacity to receive only. Relational-interactive power is greater in that it includes both transmitter and receiver capacities.[8]

Omnipotence and All-Embracing Love

Another reason for accepting a relational conception of power as the highest form of power is that a relational conception of divine power is entirely consistent with belief in all-embracing divine love. By contrast, where omnipotence is taken to mean that God transmits wholly determinative influences while receiving absolutely no influence, there are only self-refuting ways of affirming that we are loved by God. Where immutability means receiving zero influence, it denies the mutual relatedness essential to love.

Like the highest conceivable form of power, the highest conceivable form of love is relational. Love is interactive, passive and active, not just active. Love is transceiving, receiving and transmitting, not transmitting without receiving.

When we speak of loving another person, according to Ogden, we understand that love has two essential aspects: acceptance of the beloved such that s/he makes a partly determinative difference to the lover, and action toward the beloved "on the basis of such acceptance" (FF, 83–84). Divine love, says Ogden, has "these same essential aspects" (FF, 84). Ogden says:

Accordingly, as different as God's love would certainly have to be from our own, or any other merely creaturely love, it could nevertheless be conceived to be like them in having these same essential aspects: first, the acceptance of others—in God's case, the unlimited acceptance of all others—and then, secondly, action directed toward all others on the basis of such unlimited acceptance. (FF, 84)

Universal acceptance and universal action based on such acceptance are two essential aspects of "all-encompassing love" (FF, 89).

The two essential aspects of all-encompassing love are also the essential aspects of omnipotence. Ogden holds that God is "the one to whom all things make a [partly determinative] difference" (FF, 85, 88), and the one who "makes a [partly determinative] difference to all things" (FF, 88). Being made partly different by all things is universal acceptance, and making partial differences to all things on the bases of such acceptance is universal action. Universal acceptance and universal action are the essential aspects of both omnipotence and all-embracing love.

The distinction between omnipotence and all-embracing love is a matter of emphasis, not actual or possible difference. When emphasizing universal action, we tend to speak of omnipotence. When emphasizing universal acceptance, we tend to speak of all-embracing love. Omnipotence and all-embracing love are emphatically distinct ways of speaking about the same ultimate reality.

7

Toward a Metaphysics of Ethics

Temporal Process in the Metaphysics of Nature

Like *metaphysics, metaethics* has a variety of meanings. Here metaethics means analysis which seeks to describe formal features of ethical deliberation. Where metaethics focuses on those formal features which are essential to any and all ethical deliberation, that metaethical study can be described as a metaphysics of ethics or, in more traditional terminology, as "a metaphysics of morals."[1] This chapter's contribution to a metaphysics of morals is instructed by a metaphysics of nature, especially by necessary aspects of time explicated by Whitehead.

Whitehead's *The Concept of Nature* includes a chapter called "Time" (chapter 3). Here Whitehead holds that "Nature is a process" (CN, 53). Whitehead holds that the "process of nature" consists of passing "events." Passing events have continuity because each event "extends" over subsequent events, just as it was extended over by previous events. Whitehead says:

The continuity of nature arises from extension. Every event extends over other events, and every event is extended over by other events. (CN, 59)

Extended-over and partly determined events extend over and partly determine subsequent events. Whitehead says this "process of nature can also be termed the passage of nature" (CN, 54). The passage of nature, rendering all things temporal, is a temporal process.

In *Process and Reality*, Whitehead interprets necessary temporal process in terms of "becoming" (which includes and exceeds "being") and "perishing." In his essay about *Process and Reality* entitled "Process and Reality," Whitehead prescribes philosophical attention to "a trinity of three notions: being, becoming, and perishing" (ESP, 117). Whitehead's analysis of "becoming" and "perishing" necessitates a metaphysical doctrine of "objective immortality" (PR, 60). Whitehead describes the connection between "becoming," "perishing," and "objective immortality" by saying:

> Almost all of *Process and Reality* can be read as an attempt to analyze perishing on the same level as Aristotle's analysis of becoming. The notion of the prehension of the past means that the past is an element which perishes and thereby remains an element in the state beyond, and thus is objectified . . . as we perish we are immortal. (ESP, 117)

Whitehead says, the world "is always becoming, and as it becomes, it passes away and perishes" and "in perishing it yet remains an element in the future beyond itself" (ESP, 117). Because "the future inherits from the past" (PR, 350), our actions perish "and yet live for evermore" (PR, 351). Whitehead says "the creature perishes and is immortal" (PR, 82). By making partly determinative differences to the future, we attain objective immortality.[2]

By consulting the most basic form of experience—"simple physical feeling"—and finding each feeling is a "feeling which feels another feeling" (PR, 236), Whitehead discerns a necessary temporal process of becoming and perishing that is continuous, one directional, irreversible, and cumulative (PR, 237). Whitehead says:

> This passage of the cause into the effect is the cumulative character of time. The irreversibility of time depends on this character . . . there is a vector character which transfers the cause into the effect. (PR, 237)

And Whitehead finds there are necessary distinctions between past, present, and future.

In his chapter on "Past, Present, Future," Whitehead says the past "has an objective existence in the present which lies in the future beyond itself" (AI, 191). A present experience is a transistional moment partly determined by past experiences and partly determinative of future experiences.

> Each moment of experience confesses itself to be a transition between two worlds, the immediate past and the immediate future. (AI, 192)

Each transitional moment of experience, being only partly determined by previous experiences, introduces its own measure of "novelty" or "creativity." "Creativity," says Whitehead, "expresses the notion that each event is a process issuing in novelty" (AI, 236). As the "many become one, and are increased by one," there is a continuing "creative advance" (PR, 21). The continuous, one-directional, irreversible temporal process of creatively passing inheritances from the past into the future is a necessary, unconditional, universal feature of reality.

"Pantemporalism" labels the view that temporal process is a metaphysical necessity. For process philosophy, "pantemporalism" and "panexperientialism" are one. Whitehead conceives of an "event" as "a process whose outcome is a unit of experience" (SMW, 177). Since all actualities experience and since experiencing is a temporal process, panexperientialism entails pantemporalism. Griffin says:

since we hold that *all actualities are units of experience* and that a plurality of such actualities necessarily exists, we hold that *time exists necessarily*, not as a contingent emergent. ("Actualities" here refers to genuine individuals, not aggregates. . . .)

Accordingly, process philosophy's *pantemporalism and its panexperientialism are ultimately one and the same thing*. . . . (PUST, 11; italics added)

Process philosophy's panexperientialism refutes the modern scientific doctrine which holds that nature is mostly composed of inert, unexperiencing, and uncreative bits of matter. Similarly, process philosophy's pantemporalism refutes recently popular claims that modern relativity physics exhibits timeless realities without distinctions between past, present, and future.

A Whiteheadian refutation of the "fundamental premise of the timelessness of physics" (vii) is presented in *Physics and the Ultimate Significance of Time*, edited by Griffin. Here, process philosophers and physicists dialogue about the metaphysical status of time. According to my reading of this dialogue, modern physics fails to show that pantemporalism is actually or even possibly false. Like panexperientialism, pantemporalism is a metaphysical doctrine affirmed by every actual experience-experiment and denied by no actual or possible experience-experiment.[3]

A Formal Analysis of Ethical Deliberation Explicitly Attentive to Necessary Temporal Distinctions

In his chapter entitled "Philosophic Method," Whitehead says "theory dictates method," and he illustrates the power of theory to dictate method by reference to his own doctrine of "the transient aspect of nature" (AI, 220). Here I employ Whitehead's doctrine of the "transient aspect of nature" as a theory dictating method in analyzing ethical deliberation. The transient aspect of nature dictates parsing ethical deliberation according to necessary temporal distinctions.

Like Whitehead, Hartshorne prescribes philosophical attention to temporal distinctions. To be sure, "temporal distinctions" is Hartshorne's wording in *Creative Synthesis and Philosophic Method* where he holds "temporal distinctions are modal [necessary] distinctions" (62). Attention to necessary aspects of temporal process (time) is a Whiteheadian (process) and Hartshornean (neoclassical) requirement for an adequate metaphysics, including an adequate metaphysics of nature and an adequate metaphysics of ethics.

It is consistent with Whitehead and Hartshorne to hold, as I do, that all ethics is social ethics. Where ethics is about any actual or possible experience, ethics is about social relations. Whitehead's feeling of feeling (PR, 236) and his many becoming one increased by one (PR, 21) are social-relational conceptions of experience. Similarly, Hartshorne's "Philosophy of Shared Creative Experience" (CSPM, 1) is a social-relational conception of experience. Hartshorne presents a "Social Conception of the Universe" in *Reality as Social Process*. And he presents "A Social Conception of God" in *The Divine Relativity*. Reality is social. Rendering this point explicit is one of the gains in qualifying "ethics" with "social." Another gain in speaking of ethics as social ethics is the implication that ethics includes possible recourse to social science.

Social science presupposes a metaphysical truth about time and temporal distinctions clearly accounted for in the philosophies of Whitehead and Hartshorne—namely this: *Past events are partly determinative of present events which are partly determinative of future events.*

Given this metaphysical truth, a social-historical description of the past is understood to have partly determinative implications for the present, and a sociological description of the present is understood to have partly determinative implications for the future. Social scientific descriptions have at least implicit predictive power. Thus, forms of social ethical analysis having a social scientific component include these distinct elements: (1) *interpretative themes*, (2) *populations* or *circles of concern*, (3) *descriptions*, (4) *predictions*, (5) *visions* (alternative predictions), and (6) *prescriptions*. Each element is permeated with (7) *values* and *value judgments*.[4]

Interpretative themes are selected based upon value judgments about what is important, good (or bad), and worthy (or unworthy) of attention. According to Whitehead, there are no uninterpeted facts. Whitehead says:

If we desire a record of uninterpreted experience, we must ask a stone to record its autobiography. Every scientific memoir in its record of the 'facts' is shot through and through with interpretation. (PR, 15)

. . . there are no brute, self-contained matters of fact, capable of being understood apart from interpretation as an element in a system. (PR, 144)

Fundamental value judgments lead us to interpret the world in terms of selected aspects, features, typologies, and themes.

Social science and social ethics are studies pertaining to selected *populations* or *circles of concern*. Social scientific *descriptions* are usually descriptions of selected human populations. Human populations are frequently distinguished by reference to time span, geographic location, and other partly empirical-historical and partly existential-historical distinctions such as tribal, national, and ethnic identities.[5] That part of social science which describes the past and the past's contributions to the present is commonly called history. That part of social science which describes the present, or more precisely, the recent past, is commonly called sociology.

Sociology, insofar as it is a science rather than a mere academic account of what's new, goes beyond simply reporting old and recent news. In addition to offering descriptions of the present and of the past's contributions to present events, sociology offers *predictions*. Social scientific predictions are about probable future events following from present and past trends and influences.

Social ethics reaches beyond social science by including explicit and sustained attention to evaluating descriptions and predictions, and to formulating *prescriptions*.[6] Social ethical prescriptions are guided by value-laden *visions* of more righteous alternative futures. Envisioning more righteous alternatives (alternatives to continuing along the present path into the most probable future) is inherently critical of circumstances, habits, and policies contributing to the predicted (most probable) less righteous future. Such visions favor social ethical prescriptions contributing to future realizations of more righteous alternatives.[7] Social ethical prescriptions concern what we should be doing in order to make more righteous differences to the probable future. All ethical deliberation is founded upon the metaphysical presupposition that being, becoming, doing, or merely thinking differently makes at least some difference to the future, and upon the metaethical presupposition that we ought to value some differences over others, namely those differences contributing to future realizations of more righteous alternatives.[8]

The Necessity of God in Ethics

According to neoclassical thinking, metaphysical theological truths are necessary for coherent moral theory. In "God and Righteousness" (MVG, chapter 4), Hartshorne holds that ethics needs theology because ethics needs reference to a supreme instance of righteousness (divine goodness) and a supreme instance of love (divine love).

In *The Divine Good: Modern Moral Theory and the Necessity of God*, Franklin Gamwell follows Hartshorne in arguing that for all coherent moral theory, the all-inclusive divine good is "the comprehensive variable that identifies the good as such" (178). The divine good is the necessary ultimate reference against which less inclusive goods are measured. Gamwell says:

> Since I have argued that *the realization of greater or lesser good can be identified only by the concrete comparisons within the divine relativity*, to call a more creative activity better means precisely that it contributes more to the supreme diversity that is unified in the activity of God. (DG, 182; italics added)

> The "will" of God, we may say, refers to the successive decisions of the divine, and, since *the greater or lesser goodness of all activities can only be measured within the comparison of some divine activity*, that which God always "wills" must also define the good. (DG, 182; italics added)

Gamwell holds that "the comprehensive variable or measure in accord with which all actualities may be compared and thereby evaluated as better or worse" (DG, 168) is the divine good. The divine good is no mere abstraction. It is the concrete divine actuality. According to the neoclassical metaphysics of Hartshorne and Gamwell, fully adequate moral theory is impossible without theology, that is, without reference to the all-inclusive, comprehensive, and variable actuality called "the divine good."[9]

Where its necessary features are rendered fully explicit, ethics is always revealed to be theological social ethics. And where also its contingent features are explicated, ethics is always revealed to be theological social ethics of some contingent and particular kind, such as, for example, black theological social ethics. Making value judgments about alternative partial goods is the essence of ethical deliberation. Logically, measuring any part of the whole requires references to other parts and to the whole. Similarly, measuring the value of any partial good requires references to alternative partial goods, and to the one all-inclusive good—the divine good.[10]

8

Epilogue:
Toward a Fully Adequate
Postmodern Theology

A fully adequate postmodern theology must explicate the following:
(1) the unconditional necessities of strict metaphysical theology,
including especially a doctrine of God as the God of all creation; (2) the
conditional or hypothetical necessities of liberation theology, including
especially a doctrine of God as the God of the oppressed; and (3) various contingencies, including especially our various actual and possible
connections to transatlantic slavery, black Atlantic experiences, colonialism, and other modern oppressions. By drawing, seeing, hearing,
feeling, and recognizing connections between ourselves and actual
enslaved and oppressed individuals, the abstractions "oppressed" and
"God of the oppressed" are given content appropriate to actual, concrete relatives.[1] Additionally, a fully adequate postmodern theology
must explicate (4) evaluative judgments about the significance and
righteousness of actual and possible past and present social relations,
as well as possible future relations, and (5) social ethical prescriptions
for making liberating differences.

In addition to the legacies of transatlantic slavery, there are other
important modern oppressions to be overcome. These other oppres-
sions include: genocide and ethnic cleansing against aboriginal and
migratory peoples, tribes, and nations, including especially the first
nations of the New World; exploitation and destruction of nonhuman

creatures and creations; and male oppression of females and children. No less than these others, patriarchy is characteristic of modernity. And overcoming it is essential to the postmodern work of transcending modernity.[2]

Obviously, this book is nowhere near being a fully adequate postmodern theology. Its most important contribution to postmodern inquiry is its argument for recognizing the essential influences of transatlantic slavery and black Atlantic experiences in the formation of modern selves, modern worldviews, and modern world orders. Then, I make another contribution to postmodern inquiry by drawing upon neoclassical metaphysics and black liberation theology to develop a black Atlantic account of strictly and broadly metaphysical aspects of struggle, power, and ethical deliberation. Now I conclude with an evaluative word about metaphysical and liberationist contributions to postmodern theology.

Neoclassical metaphysics teaches that God is the all-inclusive, all-powerful, all-embracing, all-experiencing, all-knowing, and all-loving God of all creation. This is "good news" to all creation.

Black theology teaches that, given actual experiences of being oppressed, the God of all creation is also the God of the oppressed. And from black Atlantic experiences, we learn that struggle for freedom is an inevitable response to experiencing oppression. Black theology attributes this to the omnipresent influence of divine inspiration. God's omnipresent influence is good news to the whole of creation and especially good news to the oppressed.

The more inclusive good news is required of any fully adequate postmodern theology. Where theology embraces merely universal good news, it specifies nothing about our connections to the commodified human cargo whose formative influences are essential to the birth and development of modernity. And without these mothership connections, theology cannot be adequate to black Atlantic criteria for describing, evaluating, and overcoming modernism and modernity.[3]

Moreover, merely universal good news fails to qualify as a specifically Christian gospel. The word "gospel" derives from old English "godspell" meaning "good spell" or "good news." And "good news" is the more recent English translation of the New Testament Greek "euangelion," from which comes "evangelist," meaning one who brings good news. According to biblical scriptures, evangelizing under the inspiration of "the Spirit of the Lord" means bringing "good news to the poor" (Luke 4:18) and "good news to the oppressed" (Isaiah

61:1), not just "good news" addressed to no specific populations.[4] Without specific liberating references to the actual poor and oppressed, merely universal good news is not good enough to equal the good news proclaimed by Jesus—good news to all, especially to the poor and oppressed.

Appendix A:
What is Metaphysics?

Metaphysics derives from the Greek phrase *meta ta physika* meaning "after the physical" or after the physical things of nature.[1] Classical Greek scholars used this phrase to refer to the work of Aristotle (384–322 B.C.E.), specifically those writings in a collection coming after writings on physical, natural things. Over the following centuries, *meta ta physika* became a single word—*metaphysics*—with a variety of new meanings. Today, the meanings of metaphysics are various in the extreme.

Polar Opposite Meanings

Two of the meanings of metaphysics are polar opposites. If we visualize ourselves at the midpoint of a horizontal pole or line segment where moving in one direction moves toward increasing certainty, and moving in the opposite direction moves toward increasing uncertainty, we find "metaphysics" at both ends.

Moving along the pole in the direction of increasing certainty, passing through the relative certainties and probable truths of physics and other natural sciences, when we approach the certainty end of the line segment, we discover "metaphysics." Here "metaphysics" means the study of logically certain truths about existence or reality as such.

Hartshorne identifies "something exists" as an example of a metaphysical truth. According to Hartshorne, "something exists" is contradicted by no conceivable experience and affirmed by "any experience whatever," and "nothing exists" is "nonsense" (DL, 382). Furthermore, in the process of testing the hypothesis "that 'nothing exists' and 'something exists' are both logically possible propositions" (DG, 110), Gamwell demonstrates that "something exists" is not only logically possible, but also logically necessary (DG, 111, 159), and that "nothing exists" is self-refuting (DG, 112). "Something exists" is a metaphysical truth. A metaphysical truth is a logically necessary existential truth—a logically necessary truth about existence or reality as such.[2]

Moving in the opposite direction along the line segment, and passing again through the midpoint, as we near the opposite end, we discover "metaphysics" again. Here "metaphysics" means the study of paranormal claims, claims with uncertain truth-values that are normally taken to be factually false (paranormal instead of normal). For example, the study of claims about ghosts is popularly understood to be a kind of metaphysical inquiry.

At one end, studying the claim "ghosts exist" is "metaphysics," where metaphysics means the study of contingent and doubtful paranormal claims to factual truth.[3] At the polar opposite end, studying the claim "something exists" is also "metaphysics" where metaphysics means the study of logically certain truths about existence as such. In this book, "metaphysics" refers to logical certainty.

Here, it is important to note that strict *metaphysical claims are claims to logical certainty, not epistemological certainty*. Gamwell distinguishes between "logical and epistemological certainty," and he holds that the latter is impossible, and that the former is characteristic of valid metaphysical claims (DG, 93, 107). Similarly, Hartshorne denies epistemological certainty to metaphysical inquiry. Hartshorne says:

> Locke was particularly, and rightly, concerned about the supposed certainty of the innate ideas. But it was accidental and irrelevant if the rationalists identified 'a priori' with 'certain'. That any experience, *to sufficient reflection*, illustrates the metaphysical conceptions is no guarantee that a given individual at a given time has so reflected as to be 'clear and distinct' or certain about his formulation of the conceptions. Formulation, verbalization, is an art, and a fallible one whose success is a matter of more or less. . . . Mistakes are possible in mathematics and formal logic; is not metaphysics just the part of *a priori* knowledge in which clarity and certainty are least readily attained? Intellectual history suggests that this is so. . . . Accordingly, 'a priori,' or 'innate,' is one thing, and 'certainly known' is quite another. If what a man most wants is certainty he might better turn his attention to arithmetic, elementary logic, or even some parts of natural science, than to metaphysics. (CSPM, "What Metaphysics Is," 31–32)

In contrast to contingent (nonnecessary) factual claims, metaphysical claims are "said to be logically necessary and, in that sense, invariable or certain" (DG, 93).

Strictly defined, metaphysics is the scientific study (searching for, constructing, analyzing, examining, testing, validating) of logically necessary existential truths—logically necessary truths about existence or reality as such.

Necessary Truth and Contingent Fact, A Priori and A Posteriori Methods

Distinguishing between necessary truths and nonnecessary or contingent truths is essential to distinguishing metaphysics from other scientific inquiry. Gottfried Wilhelm von Leibniz (1646–1716) says, "A truth is necessary when the opposite implies contradiction; and when it is not necessary it is called contingent."[4] Leibniz distinguishes between necessary truths and contingent truths, and he refers to contingent truths as "truths of fact."[5] Physics and other natural sciences are concerned with contingent (nonnecessary) or factual truths. Metaphysics is concerned only with necessary (noncontingent) truths.

All metaphysical truths are necessary truths, but not all necessary truths are metaphysical truths. In addition to necessary truths about existence or reality as such, there are other kinds of necessary truths, including the necessary truths of math and geometry. That "all right angles are equal to each other" is Leibniz's example of the latter kind of necessary truth.[6] The necessary truths of concern to metaphysics are about reality as such.[7]

Unlike a necessary truth, a factual truth is unnecessary-contingent-conditional. For example, consider hearing it truthfully said that "the sky is blue." This factual truth is contingent upon time of day, sunlight, atmospheric conditions, and other factual conditions without which the sky could be other than blue, perhaps gray or black. The sky is blue if certain contingencies obtain. Since the sky is not necessarily blue, an empirical observation is needed for inquiry into this contingent factual matter.

Empirical method appeals to publicly verifiable or publicly falsifiable experiences or experiments.[8] Accordingly, we verify or falsify the claim for a blue sky by observing the sky and having the sensory experience of seeing or not seeing blue. Because empirical verification or falsification of a contingent factual claim awaits the outcome of particular observations or experiments, empirical validation is called *a posteriori* method. *A posteriori* is Latin for "from what is posterior" or "from what comes after" or behind. By contrast, *a priori* is Latin meaning "from what is prior" or "from what comes before."[9]

In contrast to the empirical or a posteriori method of validating contingent-factual claims, an a priori method validates claims to necessary truth. Consider again Leibniz's example, that right angles are equal to each other. We can validate claims for the equality of right angles prior to doing empirical measurements of objects with right angles. Prior to receiving data from measuring such objects, an a priori deliberation can show that the equality of right angles is logically necessary given the meaning of what constitutes a right angle. The meaning of a right angle is such that any claim for the inequality of right angles is self-contradictory and nonsensical.

Similarly, contradicting the metaphysical truth that "something exists" yields self-contradiction. It makes no sense for me to say "nothing exists" because I contradict myself with an implicit witness to my own existence and to the existence of whoever I am speaking to. Every actual experience and every actual witness affirms the existence of something, and no actual or possible experience or witness could do otherwise. The truth of claims for the necessary existence of something and the necessary equality of right angles can be known by way of an a priori analysis showing that all contradictory statements, such as "nothing exists" and "right angles are not equal," are self-refuting or self-contradictory and hence nonsense.

An a priori method of distinguishing a statement of necessary truth from factual statements begins with formulating a contradictory statement. Given a coherent and meaningful statement "x," if a contradictory statement "not x" has coherent meaning, the contradicted statement "x" is factual, either factually true or factually false. If it is impossible to formulate a contradictory statement with coherent meaning because every possible formulation of "not x" is self-refuting, then the uncontradictable statement is a necessary truth.[10]

In *Creative Synthesis and Philosophic Method*, Hartshorne's first sentence in "What Metaphysics Is" (chapter 2) says, "Metaphysics may be described as the study which evaluates a priori statements about existence" (19). A priori statements about existence (a priori existential statements) are statements that do not negate any actual or possible observation, experiment, or experience, and they are unavoidably and necessarily affirmed (at least implicitly) by every actual or possible observation, experiment, or experience.[11] Also, Hartshorne defines metaphysics as inquiry into "what is common to all possibility" (DR, xvi).

Formulating Non-restrictive Existential Statements

The "unrestrictive" character of metaphysical statements is emphasized by Hartshorne in "Non-restrictive Existential Statements" (CSPM, chapter 8). Here Hartshorne holds that metaphysical statements are "completely non-restrictive" statements about existence. For example, "something exists" is restrictive of nothing whatever. "Something exists" is a purely positive assertion. By contrast, factual statements are "partially restrictive" of existential possibilities. Hartshorne says:

Ordinary factual statements are partially restrictive of existential possibilities: for, if they are affirmative, they also implicitly deny something; and if they are negative, they also implicitly affirm something. Thus, 'There are men in the room' denies that the room is filled solid from floor to ceiling with nonhuman bodies; and 'There are no men in the room' affirms that every substantial part of the room contains something (if only air, or a 'vacuum' furnishing free passage to radiant energy) other than a man. (CSPM, 159)

A factual statement is conditionally true (or false) and partly restrictive. A metaphysical statement is unconditionally true and completely non-restrictive. Hartshorne says metaphysics is "the subject which tries to formulate *non-restrictive or necessary existential truths*" (CSPM, 172; italics added).

In addition to "completely non-restrictive" statements and "partially restrictive" statements, there are also "completely restrictive" statements. A completely restrictive statement, says Hartshorne, "denies that any existential possibility is realized" (CSPM, 159). It is a wholly negative assertion. "Nothing exists" is a completely restrictive statement. A completely restrictive statement can be verified by no actual or conceivable experiment or experience, and moreover, it is falsified by every actual and any conceivable experiment or experience. A completely restrictive statement, says Hartshorne, "expresses an impossibility, not a conceivable but unrealized fact" (CSPM, 159). Completely restrictive statements are absurd-nonsense-meaningless.

As a consequence of excluding completely restrictive (wholly negative) statements from meaningful discourse, we are left with two kinds of meaningful statements about existence: partly restrictive statements (factual statements) and completely non-restrictive statements (metaphysical statements). According to Hartshorne's "principle of the partial positiveness of every fact" (CSPM, 160), every factual statement is partly positive and (at least implicitly) partly negative-restrictive. By contrast, metaphysical statements are wholly positive and completely non-restrictive.

Observational Falsifiability as Criterion

Because metaphysical statements are completely non-restrictive, they can be falsified by no observation. By contrast, factual statements can be falsified by some conceivable contrary observation. For instance, the factual claim that "the sky is now blue" can be falsified by observing an orange-red sky, but no observation can falsify the metaphysical claim that "something exists." Moreover, any observation unavoidably affirms that "something exists." Hartshorne says, *"Metaphysical truths may be described as such that no experience can contradict them, but also such that any experience must illustrate them"* (LP, 285; italics added). Metaphysical statements are confirmed as true by every observation, and they are falsified by no observation.

For Hartshorne, "observational falsifiability" (the possibility of being falsified by some conceivable observation) is the criterion for distinguishing empirical-factual statements from metaphysical statements (CSPM, 19). Drawing upon Sir Karl Popper, in "What Metaphysics Is" (CSPM, chapter 2) Hartshorne says:

I agree entirely with his [Popper's] claim that it is observational falsifiability which alone distinguishes empirical from metaphysical or a priori statements. This is a precious contribution to philosophical wisdom. (CSPM, 19)

Hartshorne says observational falsifiability alone distinguishes empirical-factual statements from metaphysical statements.

There is an exception to this Hartshornean way of distinguishing factual from metaphysical statements. In response to Hartshorne, Ogden points out that strictly speaking, "I exist" is not observationally falsifiable.[12] Although my existence is contingent-conditional-factual, nevertheless, I can never observe my nonexistence. Thus, the criterion of observational falsifiability admits a contingent statement—"I exist"—into metaphysics.

Strict Metaphysics and Metaphysics More Broadly Conceived

Because the criterion of observational falsifiability admits contingency into metaphysics, Ogden distinguishes between a *strict metaphysics* which excludes all contingent statements, and *metaphysics more broadly conceived* so as to admit a contingent statement that is in principle not observationally falsifiable—"I exist." Metaphysics in the *broad sense* is named *"metaphysica specialis"* [or "special metaphysics" (Ogden, 1985, p. 94)] because, along with completely general truths (for example, "something exists"), it includes "I exist" and related truths specific to human experience. Metaphysics in the *strict sense* is named *"metaphysica generalis"* because it includes only completely general truths (Ogden, 1975).

For *metaphysica specialis* (metaphysics in the broad sense), the criterion for truth is "unavoidable belief or necessary application *through human experience*" (Ogden, 1975, p. 48; italics added). For *metaphysica generalis* (metaphysics in the strict sense), the criterion for truth is "unavoidable belief or necessary application *through experience as such*, even divine experience" (Ogden, 1975, p. 48; italics added; also 1985, pp. 93–94).[13]

Factual and Metaphysical Statements about God

Some statements about God are factual, and some are metaphysical. Consider the following contrast between a factual statement about God and a metaphysical statement about God.

"God parted the Red Sea" is a factual statement. As a factual statement, it is true only under certain contingent conditions. Temporal location and geological events are among the contingent conditions upon which the truth-value of this factual statement depends. Prior to the creation of planet Earth and the subsequent formation of a Red Sea, statements about God actually parting the Red Sea in the past could not have been true. "God parted the Red Sea" is a factual statement, and as such, it is contingently true (or contingently false).

By contrast, "there is only one true God" is a metaphysical statement. It is necessarily true. Its necessity flows from logical analysis of the concept of God. Essential to the concept of God is the idea that God is all-inclusive. Logically and necessarily, the all-inclusive actuality (God) must be the only all-inclusive actuality. Only one actuality (the all-inclusive one) includes all actualities. Statements to the contrary are self-contradictory. Talk of more than one actuality including all actualities, like talk of no actuality including all actualities, is self-contradictory. Excluding more than one and zero, we are left with one. The all-inclusive "divine actuality"[14] is unique. This is a metaphysical truth—a logically necessary existential truth, a logically necessary truth about existence or reality as such.

Appendix B:
What is Theology?

Theology is the study of *logos* about *theos*. It seeks to find, interpret, evaluate, and construct logical-rational-thoughtful-worded deliberations about God, usually written.[1] There are many theological writings, many methods of study, and hence, many theologies.

In part one—"God"—of the *Summa Theologica*, St. Thomas Aquinas (c. 1225–1274) described all other sciences as "handmaidens" for the most noble science of sacred doctrine. Here St. Thomas distinguished between (a) theology as part of sacred doctrine "revealed by God" and "accepted through faith," and (b) "theology which is part of philosophy" and "investigated by reason."[2] Today, the theology which is part of philosophy is called "philosophical theology."

Philosophical Theology and Rules of Academic Engagement

The modern English word *philosophy* derives from joining the classical Greek words *philos* and *sophia*, meaning "love" and "wisdom," to mean "love of wisdom." The *Random House Dictionary of the English Language* (1973) defines philosophy as "**1.** the rational investigation of the truths and principles of being, knowledge, or conduct. **2.** any one of the three branches, namely natural philosophy, moral philosophy, and metaphysical philosophy, that are accepted as composing this study . . ." (1082).

Each of the various scientific disciplines in the modern university is part of philosophy where philosophy is broadly conceived as rational inquiry into *natural, moral, and metaphysical aspects of existence*. Accordingly, a Ph.D. (*Philosophiae Doctor* in Latin) in any of the

81

scientific university disciplines is a Doctor of Philosophy. Where theology is part of philosophy, it is committed to formal and informal rules of engagement shared with other modern university-compliant scientific disciplines.

These rules include obligation to *accept no argument from external authority*. A modern philosophical argument for the existence of God is not strengthened by saying Billy Graham, John Wesley, or the Pope says so, or even the Bible tells me so. Appeal to biblical authority is acceptable for religious discourse, but not for modern theological discourse where theology is part of philosophy. Instead, like other scientific disciplines, modern philosophical theology appeals to rationality, reason, experience-experiment, empirical data, logical arguments, and other supporting evidence.

Moreover, where theology is part of philosophy, evidence cannot be of a private or exclusive nature. As with scientific inquiry throughout the university, evidence must be publicly accessible. I would be in violation of modern academic rules if I argued that "I know God loves us because an angel appeared to me in a dream last night and told me so." Even if it is true that an angel appeared to me in a dream last night and told me so, this is not acceptable evidence because it is a private experience impossible for most others to replicate through their own experience and experiments. Similarly, modern rules of academic engagement would be violated if I were to argue, "I know God loves us because I am saved, and we saved folk have a special knowledge of divine love." This being true makes no difference. The rules of modern scientific-philosophical inquiry stipulate that we allow *no appeal to private, exclusive, or special experiences in principle inaccessible to the general university public*.

Modern scientific-philosophical inquiry allows *no appeal to ad hominems*. According to modern rules of academic engagement, arguments directed toward person (from Latin, *ad*/toward *hominem*/person) or character are not relevant, regardless of truth-value. Claims about Albert Einstein's personal life (true or false, good or bad) fail as arguments for or against his theory of general relativity. In the "real world" of ordinary social-political existence, an *ad hominem* can be very relevant. But in the "ivory tower" of modern university discourse, the personal virtues and vices of the scientist are not relevant to assessing the meaning and truth-value of his or her scientific assertions. Hence, *ad hominems* are not allowed.

Modern university-compliant scholarship requires that we submit work to public scrutiny, including especially critical peer reviews. Critical evaluations serve the purposes of exposing and correcting inadequacies and errors, and of validating and advancing what is most meaningful, true, righteous, and beautiful. According to university ideals, *criticism is an essential blessing.* And it should be received and offered as such.

Ideally, scholarly criticism employs win-win scoring. Win-win scoring stands in contrast with win-lose scoring. Win-lose scoring requires that winners win at the expense of others—losers. In a "zero-sum game" such as football, when the offensive team gains six yards, the defensive team loses six yards. The offensive gain of six minus the defensive loss of six yields a sum of zero. Zero-sum games employ win-lose scoring. By contrast, university scholarship employs win-win scoring.[3]

For an imaginary example, let us suppose the following. I assert "God *is* a-b-c." My peers study this assertion, and one of them argues "God is *not* a-b-c." If after discussion and debate, we discover the evidence supports a-b-c, then one point goes to me for being correct, and one point to my peer for being corrected. My assertion has been confirmed and my peer's knowledge has been advanced because now s/he understands that God really *is* a-b-c. If on the other hand, we discover God is *not* a-b-c, then one point goes to my peer for being correct, and one point to me for being corrected. "I stand corrected" is a positive advance over continuing error. Both positive and negative criticisms serve the same positive function of advancing the knowledge of all. When scholars contend according to the rules of academic engagement, everyone wins.

Of course, the ideal of everyone winning is not always actualized. Critical discourse can yield a win-lose experience if we fail to receive and offer criticism as an honorable gift contributing to our scholarly advance. For example, sometimes I attach my ego to a selected view in such a way that criticism of my selected view is received as a criticism of my person. Under such circumstances, negative criticism is received as a personal assault (as an *ad hominem*) rather than as a blessing contributing to the advancement of knowledge. Where criticism is received or offered as an *ad hominem,* the rules of academic engagement are violated, and the joy of critical discourse is seriously endangered.

Christian Theology and Rules of Academic Engagement

In accordance with Aquinas' insight, it is important to distinguish between philosophical theologies and specifically religious theologies, including Christian theologies.[4] Some Christian theologies are firmly committed to rules of engagement governing modern university-compliant scientific disciplines. For instance, in "Theology in the University" Ogden asserts that for Christian theology in the university, "there cannot be any privileged data with respect to truth" (OT, 127). According to Ogden's revisionary understanding, Christian theology is the critical and constructive study of characteristically Christian *logos* about *theos* and ultimate reality. And, says Ogden, "its standards of reflection are the same in principle as those of any other field of study" (OT, 131).

Alternatively, some Christian theologies are guided by other rules. Walter C. Kaiser Jr. holds that "theology has its own distinctive subject matter—God; its own distinctive starting point and source of subject material—revelation; its unique method of examining its subject matter—exegesis of the Scripture in light of the witness of all the evidences, historical, cultural, scientific along with the inner testimony of the Holy Spirit; and its own criteria of scholarly excellence—accountability to the canonical text and the work of the conciliar councils. . . ." Kaiser says that while theology may not "disregard all other tests and forms of logic," it objects to "such preemptive strictures as the elimination of the supernatural from the discussion."[5]

William J. Abraham is also critical of modern philosophical approaches to Christian theology. In chapter 9 "Evangelism and Modernity" of *The Logic of Evangelism* (1989), Abraham faults modern philosophical approaches to theology for being centered on human discourse rather than God. Abraham finds that "such a posture is at best sub-Christian and at worst idolatrous," and he predicts "in the end, even modernity will become obsolete in the wake of the final fulfillment of the good purposes of God for creation and history" (LE, 208).[6]

Stanley Hauerwas is another Christian theologian critical of modern philosophical approaches to Christian theology and ethics. Hauerwas finds serious fault with modern prohibitions against appeals to authority, and he challenges appeal to a universal, university public as the criterion for truth. Hauerwas argues the truth of Christian theology is tested by appeal to the authority of churchly experiences and memories.[7]

Luis G. Pedraja offers another view of Christian theology, a view rooted in an Hispanic conception of *logos*. In chapters 3 and 4, "And the Verb Became Flesh" and "God Is a Verb," of *Jesus is My Uncle: Christology From a Hispanic Perspective* (1999), Pedraja shows that where "logos" has christological and theological applications, translating "logos" as "word" is not fully adequate. For a more adequate translation, Pedraja prescribes following the centuries old Spanish habit of translating "logos" as "verbo," meaning an explicitly active word—a verb. In the beginning was the verbal word. And the verb became flesh. Where *logos* is explicitly verbal, understanding God as *logos* explicitly indicates God is active and creative, not static.[8]

Furthermore, according to Pedraja, translating *logos* as "verbo" yields a more inclusive understanding of Christian theology. Where *logos* means verb, Christian theology is more than critical study of written words about God seeking orthodoxy (right belief). Given emphasis upon verbal *logos*, Christian theology deliberates on words, on written "ratio" and spoken "sermon," and deeds, on beliefs and practices, especially churchly practices. This Christian theology seeks orthodoxy (right belief) and orthopraxis (right action).[9]

There are many Christian theologies and many ways of parsing and classifying Christian theologies. Given this variety, theological literature can be difficult to navigate.

Among distinctions essential to making sense of contemporary theological diversity, one of the most basic is the one suggested by St. Thomas Aquinas—the distinction between philosophical theologies and specifically religious theologies. Some Christian theologies are like philosophical theologies in being committed to the same rules and criteria for meaning and truth as other modern university-compliant scientific disciplines.[10] And some Christian theologies are governed by other special rules and criteria. Sometimes the special rules and criteria supplement the rules and criteria shared by university-compliant scientific disciplines, and sometimes they contradict university-compliant rules and criteria.

Notes

Preface

1. "Black Atlantic" is wording from Paul Gilroy's *The Black Atlantic: Modernity and Double Consciousness* (Cambridge: Harvard University Press, 1993).
2. "Constructive postmodern" is wording from the introduction to each of the books in the SUNY series in Constructive Postmodern Thought, edited by David Ray Griffin. Recently, Griffin came to prefer "reconstructive postmodern" over "constructive postmodern." He now says that the "postmodernism of this series can . . . be called *revisionary, constructive*, or—perhaps best—*reconstructive*" (RSN, xi). In "Reconstructive Postmodern Theology" (2003), Griffin says that "reconstructive" is better because *re*constructive "makes clearer that a prior deconstruction of received concepts is presupposed."

Introduction to SUNY Series in Constructive Postmodern Thought

1. The present version of this introduction is slightly different from the first version, which was contained in the volumes that appeared prior to 1999.
2. The fact that the thinkers and movements named here are said to have inspired the deconstructive type of postmodernism should not be taken, of course, to imply that they have nothing in common with constructive postmodernists. For example, Wittgenstein, Heidegger, Derrida, and Deleuze share many points and concerns with Alfred North Whitehead, the chief inspiration behind the present series. Furthermore, the actual positions of the founders of pragmatism, especially William James and Charles Peirce, are much closer to Whitehead's philosophical position—see the volume in this series entitled *The Founders of Constructive Postmodern Philosophy: Peirce, James, Bergson, Whitehead, and Hartshorne*—than they are to Richard Rorty's so-called neopragmatism, which reflects many ideas from Rorty's explicitly physicalistic period.

3. As Peter Dews points out, although Derrida's early work was "driven by profound ethical impulses," its insistence that no concepts were immune to deconstruction "drove its own ethical presuppositions into a penumbra of inarticulacy" [*The Limits of Disenchantment: Essays on Contemporary European Culture* (London: New York: Verso, 1995), 5]. In his more recent thought, Derrida has declared an "emancipatory promise" and an "idea of justice" to be "irreducible to any deconstruction." Although this "ethical turn" in deconstruction implies its pulling back from a completely disenchanted universe, it also, Dews points out (6–7), implies the need to renounce "the unconditionality of its own earlier dismantling of the unconditional."

Chapter 1

1. In "Imperialism, Nuclearism, and Postmodern Theism" (GRPW, chapter 8), Griffin's thesis is that a "supernaturalistic idea of God has contributed to modern imperialism in general and to nuclearism in particular" (132).

2. Awareness of modernity's threat to planetary life is the fourth of four differences between contemporary postmodern movements and previous antimodern movements identified by Griffin in his introduction to the SUNY series in constructive postmodern thought. Concerning the first three, Griffin says the following: "First, the previous antimodern movements were primarily calls to return to a premodern form of life . . . Second, . . . the current movement draws on natural science itself as a witness against the adequacy of the modern worldview. In the third place, the present movement has even more evidence than did previous movements of the ways in which modernity and its worldview are socially and spiritually destructive" (GR, xi; VPT, xiii).

3. Griffin distinguishes between early modern and late modern theologies, and he sees constructive postmodern theology correcting early and late modern errors. Early modern theology accommodated itself to early modern scientific views of the world. Constructive postmodern theology shows that early modern theology's accommodations need to be changed because the most recent science witnesses against the early modern worldview—"pointing instead toward a postmodern worldview," says Griffin (VPT, 3). Late modern theology denied the need for appeals to public criteria. Constructive postmodern theology holds that theology must appeal to public criteria of "self-consistency and adequacy to generally accessible facts of experience" and to public policy relevance (VPT, 3).

4. Here Beardslee rejects the form of postmodernism that abandons "the quest for a vision of the whole," such as the one advocated by Jean-Francois Lyotard and called "severe postmodernism" (VPT, 64–65). Instead of severe postmodernism, Beardslee prescribes a constructive postmodern vision of the whole that is instructed by Christology and Christian appropriations of Whiteheadian philosophy, including the work of Charles Birch and John B. Cobb Jr.

(VPT, 68, 70). In "Cornel West's Postmodern Theology" (VPT, chapter 8) Beardslee favors a Whiteheadian postmodernism over West's postmodernism.

5. In "The Cultural Vision of Pope John Paul II: Toward a Conservative/Liberal Postmodern Dialogue" (VPT, chapter 6), Holland finds acute awareness of the destructive aspects of modernity in the "conservative postmodern vision of the Pope" (VPT, 96). He says, "While I am not aware that the Pope himself explicitly uses the term *postmodern,* I found constant references in his writing to the crisis of modern culture and to the birth of a new cultural form" (VPT, 97). Holland's liberal postmodern assessment of the Pope's conservative postmodernism derives from seeing "dialogue as an indispensable condition to birthing a fully postmodern culture" (VPT, 98). Holland finds that conservative postmodernism and liberal postmodernism agree "that modern culture is breaking down" and disagree "on the nature of that new cultural form and how we should midwife its birth" (VPT, 108). Holland sees postmodern features in the vision of Pope John Paul II and in emerging Catholic praxis.

6. For Ferré, the "modern ideas" and values giving rise to modern civilization were first expressed by mathematically minded early modern Renaissance figures such as Leonardo da Vinci (1452–1519, Florentine artist) and Nicolaus Copernicus (1473–1543, Polish founder of modern astronomy) (BV, 108–14), and by "nonmathematical early moderns" such as William Gilbert (1544–1603, English physicist and physician known for inquiry into electricity and magnetism), Giordano Bruno (1548?-1600, Italian Renaissance philosopher and poet), and Sir Francis Bacon (1561–1626, British philosopher) (BV, 114–20). Other "founders" of the modern worldview identified by Ferré include: Johannes Kepler (1571–1630, German astronomer and mathematician), Galileo Galilei (1564–1642, Italian astronomer, mathmatician, and physicist), Thomas Hobbes (1588–1697, Bristish philosopher and political scientist), and Rene Descartes (1596–1650, French philosopher and mathematician) (BV, 120–42). Subsequent shapers of the modern worldview identified by Ferré include: Robert Boyle (1627–1692, Irish-English chemist and physicist), Benedictus Spinoza (1632–1677, Jewish philosopher born in Amsterdam), Nicolas Malebranche (1638–1715, French philosopher), Isaac Newton (1642–1727, British mathematician and physicist), Gottfried Wilhelm Leibniz (1646–1716, German philosopher), George Berkeley (1685–1753, Irish-English philosopher), Immanuel Kant (1724–1804, German philosopher), George Wilhelm Friederich Hegel (1770–1831, German idealist philosopher), Auguste Comte (1798–1857, French positivist philosopher), Charles Robert Darwin (1809–1882, English biologist), Karl Marx (1818–1883, German social theorist), James Clerk Maxwell (1831–1879, Scottish physicist), Francis Herbert Bradley (1846–1924, English idealist philosopher), Henri Bergson (1859–1941, French philosopher), Samuel Alexander (1859–1938, Australian-English philosopher), Alfred North Whitehead (1861–1947, British mathematician and philosopher), and Albert Einstein (1878–1955, German physicist) (BV, 143–82).

7. The influence of modern science and science based technology is emphasized in Ferré's account of modernity in "Toward a Postmodern Science and Technology" (SSPV, chapter 9).

8. Here *different* means *materially* different. Formal and material meanings of modernity are distinguished by Gamwell in *The Divine Good: Modern Moral Theory and the Necessity of God* (1990). Formally, "the modern age is marked in some sense by the increasing affirmation of autonomy" (DG, 3). This modern affirmation of human autonomy holds that claims about reality "cannot be validated or redeemed by appeals to some authoritative expression or tradition or institution" (DG, 4). Instead, claims about reality can be "validated or redeemed only by appeal in some sense to human experience and reason as such" (DG, 4). Gamwell judges that the formal meaning is "*explicitly* neutral to all material differences" (DG, 7), and that most so-called postmodern efforts to get beyond the modern are concerned with some material meaning of modernity (DG, 8).

Chapter 2

1. Long's books include: *Alpha: The Myths of Creation* (1963), *The History of Religions: Essays in Understanding* (edited with Joseph M. Kitagawa, 1967), *Myths and Symbols: Essays in Honor of Mircea Eliade* (edited with Kitagawa, 1969), and *Significations: Signs, Symbols, and Images in the Interpretation of Religion* (1986). His articles are too many to list here. For a nearly complete list of publications by Long, see the website of the Harvard University Center for the Study of World Religions at <www.hds.harvard.edu/cswr/arts/LongCV.htm>. *Religion and Global Culture: New Terrain in the Study of Religion and the Work of Charles H. Long* (2002), edited by Jennifer I. M. Reid, is about Long's influence. In addition to his influence among historians of religion (Long was president of the American Academy of Religion in 1973), Long has been very influential among black theologians, especially among those who are members of the Society for the Study of Black Religion. Long is a founding member and former president (1987–1990) of the SSBR. The following articles by Long are especially important to black theology: "Why Africa Can't Be Dismissed as Merely Missionary Fodder: A Reply to Mr. Toynbee" (1961), "The West African High God: History and Religious Experience" (1964), "The Black Reality: Toward a Theology of Freedom" (1969), "Perspectives for a Study of Afro-American Religion in the United States" (1971), "Civil Rights—Civil Religion: Visible People and Invisible Religion" (1974), "The Oppressive Element in Religion and the Religions of the Oppressed" (1976), and "Assessment and New Departures for a Study of Black Religion in the United States" (1981).

2. Modern slave trading was very big business operating on a global scale. In "A Big Business," a chapter of *In the Image of God: Religion, Moral Values, and Our Heritage of Slavery* (2001), David Brion Davis identifies modern slave

traders as African, "Portuguese, Spanish, Italian, Dutch, English, French, Swedish, Danish, German, American, Cuban, and Brazilian" (152). Davis says, "very few historians have succeeded in conveying the global dimensions of a ghastly system that first united five continents as Europeans traded Asian textiles, among other commodities, for African slaves who, after surviving the horrors of the Middle Passage to North or South America, were forced to produce the sugar, coffee, tobacco, rice, indigo, and cotton that helped to stimulate and sustain modern consumer economies" (IG, 152–53). Transatlantic slave-trading voyages numbered in the tens of thousands. Davis notes that data from more than two thirds of those voyages will soon appear on *The Trans-Atlantic Slave Trade: A Database on CD-ROM* (Harvard Du Bois Institute and Cambridge University Press, 1999) with records of "at least 27,233 Atlantic slave trading voyages" (IG, 153). Also, see *Slave Ships and Slaving* (1927) by George Francis Dow.

3. Concerning the numbers, Davis says, "Though historians continue to debate the numbers, it now seems probable that from eleven to twelve million Africans were forcibly shipped out from their continent by sea. Millions more perished in African wars or raids for enslavement and in the deadly transport of captives from the interior to slave markets on the coast" (IG, 63). In the "Atlantic Slave Trade" Donald R. Wright says: "For over three and one-half centuries more Africans crossed the Atlantic than Europeans. . . . Approximately 12 million slaves left Africa via the Atlantic trade, and more than 10 million arrived. The Atlantic slave trade involved the largest intercontinental migration of people in world history prior to the twentieth century." Frequently, estimates run as high as fifty million. For example, in the *Activity Book for African American History: A Journey of Liberation* (1996) Molefi Kete Asante and Augusta Mann report estimates ranging from fifteen to fifty million (13); and according to *The African American Experience: A History* (1999) by Stephen Middleton, Charlotte Stokes, and others, "Estimates for the total number of Africans lost to the West African slave trade ranged from 25 to 50 million" (56).

4. This description of the "Middle Passage" is from *Africans in America: America's Journey Through Slavery* (1998) by Charles Johnson, Patricia Smith, and the WGBH Research Team. Similarly, in "The Atlantic Slave Trade" by Donald R. Wright, the fifth section is called "Middle Passage." Here, Wright says: "The voyage from the African coast to the Americas was called the Middle Passage. For the human cargo of slaves, it was among the most difficult sea passages ever undertaken. On average, 16 percent of the men, women, and children involved perished in transit. The typical ocean crossing might last from 25 to 60 days, depending on origin, destination, and winds."

5. This general principle—that attention to cargo and other material exchange is essential to any adequate understanding of human relations—is displayed in Long's "Cargo Cults as Cultural Historical Phenomena" (*JAAR* 42.3, September 1974). Similarly, attention to economic activity is essential to

the theological ethics of Michael Greene and Darryl M. Trimiew. See Greene's "Peace and Justice!" (2002); Trimiew's "The Renewal of Covenant and the Problem of Economic Rights: The Contributions of Daniel Elazar" (*ASCE* 20, 2000); and Trimiew's *God Bless the Child That's Got its Own: The Economic Rights Debate* (1997).

6. Long presented his view of the priority of Middle Passage cargo during lectures at the Perkins School of Theology at Southern Methodist University and at St. Luke "Community" United Methodist Church in Dallas, Texas, on February 16, 17, 18, 1998. Most of my account of Long's view of modernity comes from my notes and memory of these lectures.

7. In addition to "black" and "African" identities, many African national identities were shaped by transatlantic slavery and colonialism. For example, according to Effiong A. Esedeke's chapter on "Nigeria as a Nation" in his *Christians and Nigerian Politics* (2000), prior to British colonialism, the geographic space now identified as "Nigeria" was home to around 250 nations, no one of which was called "Nigeria," a term invented in 1897 (p. 52). For more about Nigerian politics, see "Religious Pluralism and the State: A Socio-Ethical Study of the Religious Factor in Nigeria's Politics" (1993) by Simeon Olusegun Ilesanmi.

8. A Blassingame footnote says in *Slave Mutiny: The Revolt on the Schooner "Amistad"* (1953) William A. Owens says, "They learned [to write English] quickly because the Mendians [already] had a written language" (ST, 30).

9. See Long's "Primitive/Civilized: The Locus of a Problem," in *History of Religions* 20.1–2 (August and November 1980): 43–61.

10. Gilroy says: "I want to develop the suggestion that cultural historians could take the Atlantic as one single, complex unit of analysis in their discussions of the modern world and use it to produce an explicitly transnational and intercultural perspective . . . this entails a challenge to the ways in which black American cultural and political histories have so far been conceived. I want to suggest that much of the precious intellectual legacy claimed by African-American intellectuals as the substance of their particularity is in fact only partly their absolute ethnic property . . . there are other claims to it which can be based on the structure of the African diaspora into the western hemisphere" (BA, 15.

11. Gilroy offers an account of hip-hop music as an example of how previously established shipping connections influence contemporary black Atlantic culture. In his chapter on black Atlantic music, Gilroy says that "its [hip-hop's] success has been built on transnational structures of circulation and intercultural exchange established long ago" (BA, 87). Historically, this circulatory cultural exchange between blacks in Africa, the Caribbean, the Americas, and Europe began on transatlantic shipping routes. During slavery, ships carried enslaved musicians, free musicians, and other influential human ears. Later shipping manifests would include other musical influences such as choirs,

instruments, sheet music, and then LPs and CDs. The international character of hip-hop music depends upon cultural exchanges between distant populations once mainly connected by ships and their cargo. See the chapter entitled "'Jewels Brought from Bondage': Black Music and the Politics of Authenticity" (*BA*, chapter 3). Today, space satellites and wireless digital connections are layered over air, wire, road, rail, and maritime connections. The historical progression from land, to land-and-sea, to land-sea-and-air, then to land-sea-air-outer-space-and-cyber-space, has brought increasing interconnections. Presently, from almost any earthly point, with telephone, internet, and wireless technologies, one can connect, interact, and traffic with others at virtually any other earthly point; however, even today, high percentages of all transoceanic connections and exchanges are between persons at points first connected by ships.

12. *Black Jacks: African American Seamen in the Age of Sail* (1997) by W. Jeffrey Bolster is an excellent account of black maritime experiences during the age of sails. The paper covering says: "Few Americans, black or white, recognize the degree to which early African American history is a maritime history. W. Jeffrey Bolster shatters the myth that black seafaring in the age of sail was limited to the Middle Passage. Seafaring was one of the most significant occupations among both enslaved and free black men between 1740 and 1865. Tens of thousands of black seamen sailed on lofty clippers and modest coasters. They sailed in whalers, warships, and privateers. Some were slaves, forced to work at sea, but by 1800 most were free men, seeking liberty and economic opportunity aboard ship." Also see attention to shipping, especially British shipping, in Gilroy's *There Ain't No Black in the Union Jack: The Cultural Politics of Race and Nation* (1987).

13. With notes about their travels, black transatlantic travelers consulted by Gilroy include: Phyllis Wheatley (1753?–1784, poet, born in Africa, enslaved and shipped to Boston, published poetry in England), Martin Robinson Delany (1812–1885, physician, abolitionist, pan-Africanist, born in Charles Town, raised in Pittsburg, traveled to West Africa), William Wells Brown (1814–1884, abolitionist, writer, orator, born in Chelsea, Massachusetts, lectured in England, Ireland, Scotland, Wales, France), Frederick Douglass (1817–1895, abolitionist, journalist, author, born in Maryland, traveled to England), Alexander Crummel (1819–1898, minister, abolitionist, born in New York City, traveled to England, Liberia), Anna Julia Cooper (1858–1964, educator, scholar, born in Raleigh, North Carolina, traveled to Paris), Ida B. Wells Barnett (1862–1931, journalist, antilynching crusader, born in Holly Springs, Mississippi, traveled to England), W. E. B. Du Bois (1868–1963, sociologist, born in Great Barrington, Massachusetts, traveled to the Soviet Union, Ghana), Marcus Garvey (1887–1940, black nationalist, born in Jamaica, traveled to North America, Central America, South America, England), and Richard Wright (1908–1960, novelist, born in Tennessee, traveled to France). Gilroy identifies Frantz Fanon (1925–1961, psychiatrist, political theorist, born in

Martinique, traveled to Algeria, France) and Cyril Lionel Robert James (1901–1989, political theorist, born in Trinidad, traveled to the U.S., Mexico, England) as "the two best-known black Atlantic thinkers," and he says that his failure to treat their work is an obvious omission (BA, xi). Also, for another Du Bois-instructed analysis attentive to black transatlantic travelers, see Corey D. B. Walker's "'Of the Coming of John [and Jane]': African American Intellectuals in Europe, 1888–1938," *Amerikastudien/American Studies* 47.1 (Spring 2002). Du Bois's travels are treated in "The Motif of the Stranger in *The Souls of Black Folk*" (AAR-Atlanta, 2003) by Arthur Sutherland.

14. Gilroy cites *The Philosophical Discourse of Modernity* (1987) and *Postmodernism; Or, The Cultural Logic of Late Capitalism* (1991) by Jürgen Habermas.

15. Also, see Kenneth Mostern's "Modernity, Postmodernity, Social Marginality" (circa 1995) in *CTheory* on the world wide web at <www.ctheory.com/r-modernity_postmodernity.html>. Here Mostern offers a critical review of two books: Gilroy's *The Black Atlantic,* and *Framing the Margins: The Social Logic of Postmodern Culture* (1994) by Phillip Bryan Harper.

16. Science and technology are emphasized in Ferré's account of modernity in "Toward a Postmodern Science and Technology" (SSPV, chapter 9).

17. Cobb also marks the seventeenth century. He says, "Much of modern social thought reflects the seventeenth century theory of the social compact" (SSPV, 99).

18. While 1444 is an appropriate historical marker, we should not neglect earlier contributions to the modern habit of enslaving black Africans. According to Davis, among others, pre-1444 contributions included "the Arabs' contributions" (IG, 148) such as "the development of the Arab and Berber caravan trade in gold and slaves" (IG, 158). Here Davis draws upon *The Slave Trade: The Story of the Atlantic Slave Trade, 1440–1870* (1997) by Hugh Thomas and *The Making of New World Slavery: From the Baroque to the Modern, 1492–1800* (1997) by Robin Blackburn.

19. In his February 1998 lectures to the Perkins Black Seminarians and the St. Luke "Community" UMC congregation on the significance of Middle Passage cargo, Long described his method as "inquiry into the secret of the cargo." Also, methodical concern with relations to cargo is developed in his "Cargo Cults as Cultural Historical Phenomena" (1974).

20. "Thank you" to Onais Dickson Jr. for calling attention to classical Greek and Roman slavery. See *Classical Slavery* (1999) edited by Moses I. Finley.

21. "Thank you" to Patricia Francies for calling attention to Cerami's conversation about Banneker on a 27 July 2002 cable broadcast of C-Span's *Book TV,* and to Kenneth Walker for encouraging me to write about Banneker.

22. Sirius, the brightest star in our sky, appears to be a single white star. In 1862 American astronomer Alvan Clark detected a white dwarf star in orbital relation to Sirius (*Microsoft Encarta Encyclopedia 2000*). Long before the development of powerful instruments capable of detecting that dwarf star, Ban-

neker knew it was there. How Banneker came to know this is a mystery. Cerami believes this knowledge came to Banneker by way of Dogon ancestors. The Dogon are a black African people who have long known that Sirius consists of two orbiting stars and that the orbital period is approximately fifty years. Accepting Cerami's answer transforms the mystery of Banneker's knowledge into a mystery about Dogon knowledge (BB, 184, 218–19). How could the Dogon know a visible star and an invisible dwarf were in a fifty-year orbit? The *National Audubon Society Field Guide to the Night Sky* (December 2000) describes another mystery concerning Sirius: "All the ancient sources, around 2,000 years old, describe Sirius in such terms as 'red,' 'fiery,' and 'coppery,' whereas today (and in an observation recorded about A.D. 1000) it is very white, with a tinge of blue. One suggestion is that the small companion star was a red giant only 2,000 years ago, but that seems too rapid a change on the time scale of stellar evolution, and no surrounding expelled gases have been detected. No one yet has a convincing answer to the puzzle" (Audubon, 459–60). The obvious partial answer to the mystery of Dogon knowledge is that a very long time ago the Dogon observed a fifty-year cycle of variations in the appearance of Sirius. The Audubon's account indicates that the appearance of Sirius included variations in redness and whiteness. Those ancient variations may have been cyclical, owing to the changing positions of a red or reddish star in orbital relations with a white star. Later, perhaps by 1000 C.E., the reddish star became white. And without varying red-white contrasts, cyclical variations became impossible to see. But the fifty-year timing of the now invisible cycle could be extrapolated from knowledge of ancient times when that cycle was visible. Also, see Long's treatment of Dogon cosmology with emphasis upon water symbolism (AMC, 26–27, 111–12, 188–89).

23. Contrary to Cerami, Banneker was not "alone" in holding that there are extra-solar planets (BB, 176–82). In *Astro-Theology: Or a Demonstration of the Being and Attributes of God from a Survey of the Heavens* (London: W. Innys, 1715), William Derham (1657–1735) argued it is probable that every fixed star has a system of planets (36–37). "Thank you" to Charles M. Wood for reference to Derham, and to Sandra M. Trostle for a copy of Banneker's 1793 almanac.

24. For example, consider *Steps in the Scientific Tradition: Readings in the History of Science* (1968), edited by Richard S. Westfall and Victor E. Thoren. This work includes readings from Aristotle, Ptolemy, Lucretius, Roger Bacon, Jean Buridan, Galileo Galilei, William Harvey, René Descartes, Isaac Newton, Benjamin Franklin, Antoine Lavoisier, John Playfair, Thomas Young, Sadi Carnot, Theodor Schwann, Charles Darwin, J. J. Thomson, Thomas Hunt Morgan, and Irving Langmuir, but nothing from Banneker's almanacs. This is far from unusal. Cerami says this "glaring omission occurs in every leading encyclopedia and in histories of astronomical sciences found in the Library of Congress, the Free Library of Philadelphia, and the Technology Division of the Martin Luther King Library, Washington, D.C." (BB, 237). Banneker's contributions

are treated in "Benjamin Banneker, First Man of Science" (1988) and in *The Life of Benjamin Banneker: The First African-American Man of Science: Second Edition: Revised and Expanded* (Baltimore: Maryland Historical Society, 1999, first edition 1972), both by Silvio A. Bedini. Bedini cites a November 1970 letter to the *New York Times Sunday Book Reviews* lamenting "the absence of a biographical sketch of Banneker in *The Dictionary of Scientific Biography*" (LBB, 412).

25. Knowledge of Banneker's survey work was increased when the U.S. Postal Service issued a Benjamin Banneker stamp as part of the Black Heritage series on 15 February 1980. The stamp shows Banneker with a survey instrument. "Thank you" to Linda Brown for giving me a four-stamp first-day issue (#285 of 3500) of the Banneker stamp (see the illustration of the one-stamp first-day issue in Cerami's book, p. 214) and for world wide web research on Dogon astronomy.

26. Ernest Everett Just (1883–1941) is another African-American transatlantic traveler and contributor to modern science. Just is author of *The Biology of the Cell Surface* (1939) and other important publications in biology and zoology. See Kenneth R. Manning's *Black Apollo of Science: The Life of Ernest Everett Just* (New York: Oxford University Press, 1983). Also, concerning African contributions to astronomy: In his "Thoughts Upon Slavery" (1774), John Wesley draws upon Anthony Benezet's reports about West African peoples. Here a correspondent to the Royal Academy of Sciences in Paris is quoted as saying this about one unidentified West African people: "It is amazing that an illiterate people should reason so pertinently concerning the heavenly bodies. There is no doubt, but that, with proper instruments, they would become excellent astronomers" (*The Works of John Wesley*, vol. 11, sec. 8, p. 63). As here indicated, some eighteenth century North Atlantic scholars knew that West African peoples (including the Dogon) had engaged in astronomical studies.

27. Whitehead did better. When Whitehead focused on world order as distinct from worldview, transatlantic slavery came into view (AI: 19–20, 23, 27–28). Still, even for Whitehead, transatlantic slavery was not among the defining, distinctive, or main events of modernity.

28. For an extended deliberation on the contemporary burden of our slave legacy, including a call for paying "massive restitutions" (107), see *The Debt: What America Owes to Blacks* (2000) by Randall Robinson.

29. For a few of many examples of black theological attention to the experiences and religions of North American slaves, see the following: *Cut Loose Your Stammering Tongue: Black Theology in the Slave Narratives* (1991) edited by Dwight N. Hopkins and George C. L. Cummings; *Dark Symbols, Obscure Signs: God, Self, and Community in the Slave Mind* (1993) by Riggins R. Earl Jr.; *Were You There? Godforsakenness in Slave Religion* (1996) by David Emmanuel Goatley; "'There's More in the Text than That': William Wells Brown's *Clotel*, Slave Ideology and Pauline Hermeneutics" (1997) by Abraham Smith; *Down, Up, and*

Over: Slave Religion and Black Theology (2000) by Dwight N. Hopkins; and *Down By the Riverside: Readings in African American Religion* (2000) edited by Larry G. Murphy.

30. Also, black theologies instructed by Du Bois and Long understand black American religion in transatlantic terms, as partly African-American and partly African. For example, in *The Spirituality of African Peoples: The Search for a Common Moral Discourse* (1995) Peter J. Paris says his task is "to explicate the common features implicit in the traditional worldviews of African peoples as foundational for an African and African American moral philosophy," and he makes "plausible arguments concerning the continuities of African experience on the continent and in the North American diaspora" (19). Similarly, in *Jesus Is Dread: Black Theology and Black Culture in Britain* (1998) by Robert Beckford, black British religion is understood in transatlantic terms; in *A Pan-African Theology: Providence and the Legacies of the Ancestors* (1992) and *Black and African Theologies: Siblings or Distant Cousins?* (1986), Josiah Young develops a transatlantic pan-African perspective; and in *Decolonizing Theology: A Caribbean Perspective* (1981) by Noel Leo Erskine, black Caribbean religion is understood in transatlantic terms. Also, Josiah Young draws upon Du Bois in "Dogged Strength Within the Veil: African-American Spirituality as a Literary Tradition" in *The Journal of Religious Thought*, Volumes 55.2 and 56.1 (Fall-Spring, 1999–200).

31. Gilroy is correct. When analyzing modernity, modern and postmodern scholars commonly ignore the formative influences of transatlantic slavery. In *Sources of the Self: The Making of Modern Identity* (1989) by Charles Taylor, transatlantic slavery plays no part in the making of modern identify. In *Modernity: Christianity's Estranged Child Reconstructed* (2000) by John Thornhill, modernity is described in terms of replacing traditional authority with accountability to "shared intellectual inquiry" (vii). Unlike black Atlantic scholars, Taylor, Thornhill, and many others are not instructed by Du Bois, and they ignore modern connections to Africa and transatlantic slavery.

32. See *The Nations Within: The Past and Future of American Indian Sovereignty* (1984) by Vine Deloria Jr. and Clifford M. Lytle. Also, from among other books by Deloria, see the following: *Custer Died For Your Sins: An Indian Manifesto* (1969), *God is Red: A Native View of Religion* (1973), *The Metaphysics of Modern Existence* (1979), and *Red Earth White Lies: Native Americans and the Myth of Scientific Fact* (1995).

33. In *The World and Africa* (1947), Du Bois notes that many white scholars sought to justify their "right to live upon the labor and poverty of the colored peoples of the world" by using science and history to prove that the white race was superior to others, and that "everything really successful in human culture was white. . . . In order to prove this, even black people in India and Africa were labeled as 'white' if they showed any trace of progress" (WA, 20). Also, see the following: *Stolen Legacy* (1954) by George G. M. James; *The African Origins*

of Civilization: Myth or Reality (1974) by Cheikh Anta Diop; *Africa: Mother of Western Civilization* (1981) by Yosef A. A. ben-Jochannan; and *Black Athena: The Afroasiatic Roots of Classical Civilization, Volume 1: The Fabrication of Ancient Greece, 1785–1985* (1987) by Martin Bernal.

34. The need for a more comprehensive view of modernity is acknowledged in Beardslee's call for process theology to dialogue with West, and in Cobb's call for going beyond Eurocentrism. While he disagrees with most of what West says about process theology, Beardslee maintains that process theology needs to dialogue with West because "our kind of theology needs to be pressed in the direction of the pragmatic engagement and social criticism that lie at the heart of West's work" (VPT, 153). See Beardslee's "Cornel West's Postmodern Theology" in *Varieties of Postmodern Theology*. And in his review of Frederick Ferré's *Being and Value* in *Process Studies* 28.1–2 (Spring-Summer 1999), Cobb says the following: "The greatest weakness is the limitation to the Western tradition—a weakness he [Ferré] recognizes. To the postmodern movements he mentions I would add the ending of Eurocentrism. A truly postmodern metaphysics will draw on Asian and primal understanding. Doing so could deepen Ferré's meta-ecology" (146). Also, Reiland Rabaka calls for a more comprehensive view of colonialism in "Deliberately Using the Word Colonial in a Much Broader Sense" in *Jouvert* 7.2 (Winter-Spring 2003) on the world wide web at <social.chass.ncsu. edu/jouvert/v7i2/rabaka.htm>.

35. Recently more historians are recognizing the formative influences of transatlantic slave trading and New World slavery upon the whole of modernity. Davis says that until recently, "most teachers of American history continued to regard 'Negro slavery' as a branch of local southern history. It was only in 1969 with Philip Curtin's first serious effort to compile an accurate 'census' of the entire Atlantic slave trade that an increasing number of historians began to grasp the intercontinental breadth and importance of the subject" (IG, 10). Davis notes that Curtin's *The Atlantic Slave Trade: A Census* (1969) is not limited to the United States, "a region which we now know absorbed no more than 5 or 6 percent of the African slaves brought to the New World" (IG, 15). Also, Davis describes Robin Blackburn as "the first historian to explore at some length the role of the larger New World slave system in 'the advent of modernity'" (IG, 155). See Blackburn's *The Making of New World Slavery: From the Baroque to the Modern, 1492–1800* (1997) and Hugh Thomas's *The Slave Trade: The Story of the Atlantic Slave Trade, 1440–1870* (1997).

36. The intimate connection between modern Christianity and modern slavery is made in "Spirituality and Social Transformation: Perspectives on Wesleyan and Process Theologies" by Henry James Young in *Thy Nature and Thy Name Is Love* (2001). Here Young quotes Du Bois *(The World and Africa)* as saying modern slavery was "created" and "continued" by Christians (344).

Chapter 3

1. In addition to black Atlantic sources, other neglected and excluded sources are essential to developing a more adequate account of modernity. Theological attention to the excluded is prescribed in *God and the Excluded* (2001) by Joerg Rieger.

2. Ogden explicates this important distinction between broad and strict senses of metaphysics in "The Criterion of Metaphysical Truth and the Senses of 'Metaphysics'" in *Process Studies* 5.1 (Spring 1975). In *The Divine Good* (1990) Gamwell follows Ogden by distinguishing between "pragmatically necessary" existential claims about human existence and "logically necessary" existential claims about "reality as such." Gamwell says that the study of "pragmatically necessary" existential claims is metaphysics "in the broad sense," and the study of "logically necessary" existential claims is metaphysics "in the strict sense," and that the broad sense of metaphysics is sometimes called "transcendental hermeneutics," and strict metaphysics is sometimes called "transcendental metaphysics" (DG, 160–63).

3. "Philosophers of process" is wording from the title of *Philosophers of Process* (1965), edited by Douglas Browning. Hartshorne's contribution, "The Development of Process Philosophy," is reprinted in *Process Theology: Basic Writings By the Key Thinkers of a Major Modern Movement* (1971), edited by Ewert H. Cousins. Also, Hartshorne identifies Bergson, Peirce, James, Dewey, and Whitehead as "five philosophers of process" (CSPM, xiii). Peirce, James, and Dewey are also classified as "pragmatists" (3) in *Pragmatic Theology* (1998) by Victor Anderson, and in *The American Evasion of Philosophy: A Genealogy of Pragmatism* (1989) by Cornel West.

4. See Hartshorne's comments on Greek metaphysical errors in "What Metaphysics Is" (chapter 2) and in "Present Prospects for Metaphysics" (chapter 3) in *Creative Synthesis and Philosophic Method* (1970). Hartshorne holds that Greek thought is not so much wrong as one-sided (CSPM, 277). Also, he says, "I am convinced that 'classical theism' (as much Greek as Christian, Jewish, or Islamic) was an incorrect translation of the central religious idea into philosophical categories" (DR, vii).

5. Some Whiteheadian philosophers and process theologians agree with Hartshorne in seeing the need to place equal emphasis upon "process" *and* "relativity." Accordingly, they speak of "process-relational" thought. For example, in her contribution to *Thy Nature and Thy Name is Love*, Mary Elizabeth Moore speaks of "process-relational theology" (315) and "process-relational metaphysics" (329). Similarly, relationality is emphasized in Douglas Sturm's *Solidarity and Suffering: Toward a Politics of Relationality* (1998).

6. Here I am quoting Hartshorne as quoted by Paul Weiss (EA, 113) who is quoting from "Man in Nature," Hartshorne's contribution to *Experience, Existence, and the Good* (1961), edited by Irwin C. Lieb.

7. Henri Bergson (1851–1941), Nikolai Berdyaev (1874–1946), Alfred North Whitehead (1861–1947).

8. For more about Hartshorne's view of divine creativity, see "God and Creativity" (1969) by Gene Reeves.

9. In "Why Psychicalism? Comments on Keeling's and Shepherd's Criticisms" in *Process Studies* 6.1 (Spring 1976), Hartshorne says he prefers "psychicalism" to "panpsychism" (67). Where Hartshorne says "psychicalism" or "panpsychism," Griffin says "panexperientialism" (GRPW, 5, 24). Griffin explains: "Although I sometimes employ the term 'panpsychism,' because others use it, the term 'panexperientialism' is better for the Whiteheadian position, because the term 'psyche' has two connotations that do not apply: It suggests that all individuals have *conscious* experience (which was evidently Whitehead's reason for eschewing the term), and it suggests that the ultimate units are enduring things, rather than momentary events" (RSN, 150).

10. Hartshorne also speaks of "analogical extension" in "Why Psychicalism?" in *Process Studies* 6.1 (Spring, 1976).

11. For a neoclassical criticism of a dualist account of the relations between mind (psyche) and brain (matter), see "Mind, Brain, and Dualism" in *The Journal of Religion* 61.4 (October 1981) by Philip E. Devenish.

12. Individuals feel. Some individuals (for example, human individuals) are collections of feeling individuals (for example, individual cells), not mere nonindividual collections. Nonindividual collections such as tables do not feel, but their composite cellular individuals do feel. In "Why Psychicalism?" individuals are called "singulars," and nonindividual collectives are called "crowds" and "composites."

13. The strict metaphysical status of psychicalism is challenged by Ogden's "The Experience of God: Critical Reflections on Hartshorne's Theory of Analogy" in *Existence and Actuality* (1984). While Ogden makes no claim to falsify psychicalism by reference to a contrary observation, he argues that Hartshorne's theory of analogy "is a failure" (EA, 33). For Ogden, Hartshorne's analogies are "merely symbolic rather than truly analogical" (EA, 34), and dependence upon "such analogies" yields "philosophy rather than metaphysics in the proper sense" (EA, 35). Hartshorne disagrees. In his response to Ogden, he says: "As Ogden says, I distinguish a philosophy of life, meaning human life, from metaphysics. However, I include a theory of God and psychicalism in the latter" (EA, 42). And in "Why Psychicalism?" Hartshorne says: "The case for psychicalism is so strong, in my view, that I thank anyone for attacking the doctrine. It is one of the two doctrines I am most confident of, the other being the idea of nonclassical, creationist, or indeterminist causality. Absolute exclusion of creativity and absolute exclusion of sentience from entire portions of nature are alike groundless" (69). And he affirms "argument by analogy" (72).

14. For an extended account of Hartshorne's approach to theology, see *God in Process Thought* (1985) by Santiago Sia.

15. Concerning describing the divine relativity as surrelative, Hartshorne says: "Since the relativity of the all-surpassing is a unique and supreme case, it needs a special title. I propose the terms, Surrelative and Surrelativism, for this kind of relativity and the doctrine asserting it. The letter R has the convenience of being able to suggest another feature of the theory, which is that the relativity of the surrelative is also the reflexivity of its all-surpassingness. It surpasses itself, as well as everything else; with the difference that it surpasses others simultaneously, but itself only in a subsequent state" (DR, 21–22).

16. Because Hartshornean pan*en*theism, unlike pantheism, allows conceiving of God as a living-interactive-personal individual, it is consistent with another metaphysics that emphasizes the personhood of God—Boston Personalism. In *Personalism: A Critical Introduction* (1999) Rufus Burrow Jr. favors panentheism over pantheism (39). For more about similarities between personalism and process thought, see "Wesleyan Theology, Boston Personalism, and Process Thought" by Thomas Jay Oord in *Thy Nature and Thy Name Is Love* (2001). Also, in his review of Auxier and Davies's *Hartshorne and Brightman on God, Process, and Persons* (2000), Daniel A. Dombrowski finds that the written correspondences between Hartshorne and Brightman offer reasons to speak of "Hartshorne's personalism" and of "Brightman as a process philosopher" (*Process Studies* 30.1, Spring-Summer 2001: 166–68).

17. That the concrete divine relativity includes and exceeds the abstract divine absolutes is the transcendent instance of a metaphysical truth—that in every instance, divine or not, the relative (which is concrete) necessarily includes and exceeds the absolute (which is an abstraction from concreteness). Accordingly, all factual statements about relative-contingent-concrete actualities include (at least implicitly) and exceed (by virtue of factual content) absolute-necessary-abstract metaphysical truths. For an example of a factual statement including and exceeding a metaphyical truth, consider the statement "birds fly." This phrase states a relative-contingent-concrete truth, and it includes an implicit affirmation of the absolute-necessary-abstract metaphysical truth that "something exists." In terms of information about the factual world, "birds fly" includes and exceeds (says more than) "something exists."

18. In *Existence and Actuality*, Hartshorne distinguishes between divine existence (which is necessary and unrestrictive) and divine actuality (which is contingent and partly restrictive). This distinction is also developed in *The Logic of Perfection* (1962).

19. Hartshorne is not contradicting all views of life after death; rather, he is contradicting "one extreme view," "that after death a human career goes on forever" (OOTM, 40). Griffin shows that such "subjective immortality" is not the only view of life after death, nor the only Christian view of life after death (some Christians deny life after death), and that not every view of life after death is incredible (PPS).

20. "Objective immortality" is terminology from Whitehead's *Process and Reality*. Also, in "Immortality," a chapter in *Essays in Science and Philosophy* (1947), Whitehead speaks of "the immortality of realized value" (83), and he says, "the immediate facts of present action pass into permanent significance for the Universe" (94).

21. This contrast between divine and nondivine differences is explicated by Ogden in "The Metaphysics of Faith and Justice" (Summer 1985).

Chapter 4

1. For discussion of King's contributions to the philosophy of black power, see "Martin Luther King, Jr.'s Conception of Freedom and the Philosophy of Black Power" (23–26) in my book *Empower the People* (1991). And see "Martin Luther King's Synthesis of Love-Power-Justice" (88–93) in *Dirty Hands* (2000) by Garth Kasimu Baker-Fletcher.

2. See Cone's "The Origin of Black Theology" under "Black Theology" in *The Westminster Dictionary of Christian Theology* (1983); Gayraud S. Wilmore's introduction to "Black Power and Black Theology" (part I) in *Black Theology: A Documentary History, Volume One: 1966–1979*, Second Edition, Revised (1993), edited by Wilmore and Cone; *Introducing Black Theology of Liberation* (1999) by Dwight N. Hopkins; and *Black Theology and Ideology* (2002) by Harry H. Singleton, III.

3. See "Richard Allen and the Free African Society" (80–84) in Wilmore's *Black Religion and Black Radicalism: An Interpretation of the Religious History of Afro-American People* (1984).

4. See *An African-American Exodus: The Segregation of the Southern Churches* (1991) by Katherine L. Dvorak.

5. A similar historical process of oppressive churchly praxis yielding congregational protests, separations, and reformations as independent black churches is revealed in *The Freedom of the Spirit: African Indigenous Churches in Kenya* (1997) by Francis Kimani Githieya.

6. For more about black humanism, see *By These Hands: A Documentary History of African American Humanism* (2001) by Anthony B. Pinn. And for attention to black feminist humanism, see *Black Feminist Thought: Knowledge, Consciousness, and the Politics of Empowerment* (1990) by Patricia Hill Collins.

7. In contrast to black theology's emphasis upon "liberation," black womanist theology adds emphasis upon "survival." For example, see *Survival and Liberation: A Pastoral Theology in African American Context* (1999) by Carroll A. Watkins Ali. Survival and wilderness themes are emphasized in *Sisters in the Wilderness: The Challenge of Womanist God-Talk* (1993) by Delores S. Williams. Also, see *The Habit of Surviving* (1991) by Kesho Yvonne Scott.

8. Alice Walker's antipatriarchal theology and her call for being less restrictive of erotic feelings are given in the witness of Shug—a character in her novel *The Color Purple* (1985 [originally 1982]), see especially pp.

199–204. I am indebted to Brenda Bulger Walker for introducing me to Alice Walker's work.

9. Sanders itemizes the content of Alice Walker's definition of womanist, and her differences with Walker, in "Christian Ethics and Theology in Womanist Perspective" (1989). Also, see *Sexuality and the Black Church: A Womanist Perspective* (1999) by Kelly Brown Douglas.

10. Attention to black women's literature is characteristic of black womanist thought. In *Black Womanist Ethics* (1988) Katie G. Cannon concludes that "there is no better source for comprehending the 'real-lived' texture of Black experience and the meaning of the moral life in the Black context than the Black woman's literary tradition" (90). Here Cannon is attentive to the work of Zora Neale Hurston. Hurston, Alice Walker, and Toni Morrison are frequent literary sources for black womanist theologies. Charles Long sees that Toni Morrison's religious orientation includes remembering the influences of past actualities, including horrible events about which we are silent (AAR-Atlanta, November 2003). Also, along with the Bible, Terry McMillan's *Waiting To Exhale* is a literary guide (10) for a "New Faith womanist theology" (26) developed in *New Faith: A Black Christian Woman's Guide to Reformation, Re-Creation, Rediscovery, Renaissance, Resurrection, and Revival* (2000) by Sheron C. Patterson. In addition to literature, music is also a womanist resource. For example, see "Justified, Sanctified, and Redeemed: Blessed Expectation in Black Women's Blues and Gospels" by Cheryl A. Kirk-Duggan in *Embracing the Spirit: Womanist Perspectives on Hope, Salvation and Transformation* (1997), edited by Emilie M. Townes, and *Can I Get a Witness?* (1997), edited by Marcia Y. Riggs.

11. In "Womanist Theology: Black Women's Experience," Jacquelyn Grant says, "Black women must do theology out of their tri-dimensional experience of racism/sexism/classism" (278). Here Grant draws upon bell hooks's *Feminist Theory: From Margin to Center* (1984).

12. For a womanist concern with creation, see "A Creation-Centered Christology" and "Creation as the Least of These" (85–89) in "Immanuel: Womanist Reflections on Jesus as Dust and Spirit" (chapter 4) in *My Sister, My Brother* (1997) by Karen Baker-Fletcher and Garth Kasimu Baker-Fletcher. Also, see *Sisters of Dust, Sisters of Spirit: A Creation-Centered Womanist Spirituality* (1998) by Karen Baker-Fletcher.

Chapter 5

1. A metaphysics of struggle for freedom is distinguishable from but not separable from a metaphysics of freedom. In *Faith and Freedom: Toward a Theology of Liberation* (1979), Schubert M. Ogden offers an explicitly Christian rendering of a metaphysics of freedom as a contribution to liberation theology. Ogden prescribes that liberation theologies use the metaphysical resources worked out by Whitehead and Hartshorne because process metaphysics is

"the metaphysics that takes 'freedom' as its key concept" (FF, 73). Some black and Hispanic theologies of liberation include critical and constructive appropriations of process philosophy. For examples, see the following: *The Relational Self: Ethics and Theory from a Black Church Perspective* (1982) by Archie Smith Jr.; *Hope in Process: A Theology of Social Pluralism* (1990) by Henry James Young; and *Jesus is My Uncle: Christology From a Hispanic Perspective* (1999) by Luis Pedraja. Also, see a black theology prescribing Hartshornean resources in "Theological Resources for a Black Neoclassical Social Ethics" by Theodore Walker Jr. in *Black Theology: A Documentary History, Volume Two, 1980–1992* (1993), edited by Wilmore and Cone.

2. I remember hearing Turé (Carmichael) speak on campus during my undergraduate years (1972–1976) at the University of North Carolina at Chapel Hill, and during my graduate years (1977–1983) at the University of Notre Dame near South Bend, Indiana. Also, he spoke at Southern Methodist University in Dallas, Texas, on 23 October 1986.

3. I see the black American struggle in terms of three main abolitionist movements: movements toward (1) the abolition of slavery, (2) the abolition of segregation and discrimination, and (3) the abolition of poverty. In U.S. history, the first abolitionist movement culminated in the Civil War, and the second in the Civil Rights movement. The third abolitionist movement is just now getting started. While his contributions to the second abolitionist movement are widely celebrated, we have not yet learned to celebrate King's contributions to the third abolitionist movement. In *Where Do We Go From Here: Chaos or Community?* (1967), King dreamed of a world with no poverty, and he prescribed "the total, direct and immediate abolition of poverty" (166).

4. Critical attention to the variable aspects of struggle is prescribed by William R. Jones in *Is God a White Racist? A Preamble to Black Theology* (1973).

5. In "The Holy Spirit and Liberation: A Black Perspective" in *The A.M.E. Zion Quarterly Review* 96.4 (January 1985): 19–28, J. Deotis Roberts prescribes black theological attention to "a much neglected doctrine—the doctrine of the Holy Spirit" (19). Here Roberts connects pneumatology with liberation struggle and christology.

6. For black theological and social ethical attention to Howard Thurman, see Luther Smith's *Howard Thurman: The Mystic as Prophet* (1981), Mozella Mitchell's *The Spiritual Dynamics of Howard Thurman's Theology* (1985), and Alton Pollard's *Mysticism and Social Change: The Social Witness of Howard Thurman* (1992).

7. See "Methodology in the Metaphysics of Charles Hartshorne" by Eugene H. Peters in *Existence and Actuality: Conversations with Charles Hartshorne* (1984). Also, see Peters's *Hartshorne and Neoclassical Metaphysics* (1970). "Thank you" to Gary M. Hosea for this book.

8. See "A Conscious Connection to All That Is: *The Color Purple* as Subversive and Critical Ethnography" by Cheryl Townsend Gilkes in *Embracing the Spirit* (1997).

9. See "Looking to Your Tomorrows Today: North Carolina Central University, December 16, 1994" by Mary M. Townes in *Embracing the Spirit*, and see *Trouble Don't Last Always: Emancipatory Hope Among African American Adolescents* (2003) by Evelyn L. Parker. Also in *Embracing the Spirit*, for a black Catholic womanist perspective, see "My Hope Is in the Lord: Transformation and Salvation in the African American Community" by Diana L. Hayes.

10. Discourse about future-oriented hope and expectation is not eschatology. According to Philip E. Devenish's account of Hartshorne's (and Ogden's) eschatology, "the last things with which eschatology deals are not *additional things* that happen *chronologically later*, but *ultimate features* of things that happen *now*" (17). Given an ultimate understanding of last things/eschatology, instead of a chronological understanding, discourse about future-oriented hopes and fears is "outside the subject matter of eschatology" (17). See "Hartshorne's Eschatology: Gratefully Serving God" by Devenish, in *Creative Transformation* 6.2 (Winter 1997): 17–18. Hartshorne says, "of course we should love our fellows as we love ourselves, for the final significance of their joy or sorrow is the same as the final significance of our joy or sorrow, that they will be felt by God" (OOTM, 28). Hartshorne's eschatology is about the final-ultimate significance of being felt by God in every moment. The idea "that we know ourselves to be known by God" (103) is indigenous to African-American prayer traditions, says Thomas Spann in "An Interpretation of an African-American Prayer."

Chapter 6

1. There is very little about the most general aspects of power as such in these early formulation of black power: the 31 July 1966 "Black Power Statement" in *The New York Times* by forty-eight prominent North American black clergy; *Black Power: The Politics of Liberation in America* (1967) by Carmichael (Turé) and Hamilton; *Black Power and Urban Unrest: Creative Possibility* (1967) by Nathan Wright Jr.; "Black Power" (Chapter 2) in *Where Do We Go From Here: Chaos or Community?* (1967) by King; and *The Black Power Revolt* (1968) edited by Floyd B. Barbour. This same omission characterizes Cone's work and subsequent black empowerment theologies such as: *Black Power and Black Religion: Essays and Reviews* (1987) by Richard Newman; *Black Feminist Thought: Knowledge, Consciousness, and the Politics of Empowerment* (1990) by Patricia Hill Collins; *Empower the People: Social Ethics for the African-American Church* (1991) by Theodore Walker Jr.; *Empowerment Ethics for a Liberated People: A Path to African American Social Transformation* (1995) by Cheryl J. Sanders; *Christianity on Trial: African-American Religious Thought Before and After Black Power* (1996) by Mark L. Chapman; and *Power in the Blood: The Cross in the African American Experience* (1998) by JoAnne Marie Terrell.

2. Like most North American black empowerment theologies, many Latin American liberation theologies include little explicit attention to the meta-

physical aspects of power. For example, there is no metaphysics of power in Gustavo Gutiérrez's classic *A Theology of Liberation: History, Politics and Salvation* (1971). Also, Joerg Rieger's *Remember the Poor: The Challenge to Theology in the Twenty-First Century* (1998) is a recent liberation theology offering generous attention to power and authority, but no attention to the metaphysical aspects of power. In *The Church and Morality: An Ecumenical and Catholic Approach* (1993) by Charles E. Curran, Father Curran holds that empowering the poor is part of the church's mission (83–84). But again, Curran offers no deliberation on the metaphysical aspects of power.

3. See Leibniz's *Essais de the'odice'e sur la bonte' de Dieu, la liberte' de l'homme, et l'origine du mal* (Amsterdam, 1710), translated by E. M. Huggard as *Theodicy; essays on the Goodness of God, the freedom of man, and the origin of evil* (London, 1951), as cited in "Evil, The Problem of" by John Hick in *The Encyclopedia of Philosophy* (vol. 3, 140).

4. The contrast between interacting with all individuals and interacting with some individuals is evident in *A Natural Theology for Our Time* (1967) where Hartshorne says, "Ordinary individuals, or individuals other than God . . . influence and are influenced by *some but not all* individuals" (38, italics added). In *The Logic of Perfection* (1962) Hartshorne says: "God is not a 'particular individual,' as this phrase is normally used, meaning one with a particular, limited, partly exclusive role in the universe. Particular individuals are never relevant to all others, nor are all others ever relevant to them. We 'do nothing' for George Washington; and our remote descendants can do nothing for us. But God does something for everyone, and everyone does something for God" (LP, 92).

5. The problem of evil is resolved by reconceiving divine power in *God, Power, and Evil: A Process Theodicy* (1976) by Griffin, in "Evil and Theism: An Analytical-Constructive Resolution of the So-called Problem of Evil" (1977, Ph.D. dissertation) by Philip E. Devenish, and in *God's Power: Traditional Understandings and Contemporary Challenges* (1990) by Ann Case-Winters. Also, for other reconceptions of divine power, see "The Dipolar God and Latin American Liberation Theology" (1990) by Peter C. Phan; "God, Power and the Struggle for Liberation: A Feminist Contribution" (1990) and *Divine Power: A Study of Karl Barth and Charles Hartshorne* (1986) by Sheila Greeve Davaney; *Divine Power in Process Theism: A Philosophical Critique* (1988) by David Basinger; and *To Set at Liberty: Christian Faith and Human Freedom* (1981) by Delwin Brown. In "Values, Evil, and Liberation Theology" (1979), Griffin seeks to convince liberation theologians that solving the problem of evil requires conceiving of divine power as "persuasive" and loving, not as coercive.

6. Hartshorne's attention to the religious idea of God is emphasized in "The Religious Term 'God'" (chapter 1) in *God in Process Thought: A Study in Charles Hartshorne's Concept of God* (1985) by Santiago Sia.

7. For further discussion of Hartshorne's understanding of omnipotence, see "Divine Perfection Reconsidered: Hartshorne's Innovation" by Anna Case-Winters in *Creative Transformation* 6.2 (Winter 1997): 7–11, 35.

8. Loomer describes this more inclusive capacity in terms of "greater size" (TCP, 17–18). For Loomer, unsurpassable divine power indicates unsurpassable divine size. Also, see *The Size of God: The Theology of Bernard Loomer in Context* (1987), edited by William Dean and Larry E. Axel.

Chapter 7

1. According to traditional divisions, philosophy is composed of philosophy of nature, philosophy of value (including beauty or aesthetics) and morals, and metaphysics. And metaphysical philosophy can be divided into the metaphysics of nature and the metaphysics of value and morals. "Metaphysics of morals" is language from Kant's *Foundation of the Metaphysics of Morals*.

2. Also, see Whitehead's chapter on immortality in his *Essays in Science and Philosophy* (1947). Here, in addressing "The Immortality of Realized Value," he distinguishes between the temporal "World of Activity" and the timeless "World of Value" (ESP, 79–85).

3. Putative scientific witnesses contrary to pantemporalism are mistaken interpretations of experimental data. According to Griffin's "Time and the Fallacy of Misplaced Concreteness" (PUST), mistaken interpretations of data about time are often rooted in a logical fallacy identified by Whitehead as the "fallacy of misplaced concreteness" (SMW, 51–52, 58). This fallacy occurs when we treat an abstraction from concrete actuality as if it were the concrete actuality. Griffin describes the fallacy of misplaced concreteness as treating the map "as if it were the territory, assuming that what is not on the map is not in the actual terrain itself" (PUST, 6).

4. Medical practice has each of the formal elements identified in this analysis of social ethics. This is only slightly concealed by the modern medical practice of retaining premodern Greek and Latin vocabulary. Accordingly, description is rendered as "diagnosis." Prediction is called "prognosis." And instead of a vision, modern medicine offers an alternative prognosis. An alternative prognosis derives from the predicted efficacy of the prescribed medication, treatment, or therapy. Modern medical practice is a social ethical endeavor with sickness, injury, and disease as its main interpretive themes, and health as its main valued good. Frequently medical practice is mainly focused on a population of one—the patient. Viewing medical practice as a social ethical endeavor is consistent with Black Elk's understanding of his vocation as a holy man with visions and prescriptions for healing individuals, tribes, and nations. See Neihardt's *Black Elk Speaks* (1932). In viewing medical practice as a social ethical endeavor, I was instructed by conversations with Mary Pal-

more, M.D. Also, for critical comments on our images of the physician, see William F. May's *The Physician's Covenant* (1983).

5. Selecting to be attentive to any empirical-historical distinction is an existentially evaluative and interpretive decision. In recognizing this, I am instructed by the distinction between "empirical-historical" questions about "the past in itself" and "existential-historical" questions about "its meaning for us" (39–40) in *The Point of Christology* (1982) by Ogden. Here Ogden argues that the point of christology is to answer existential-historical questions about the meaning of Jesus for us (82). In his account of the modern quest for the empirical-historical Jesus, Ogden finds that both conservative and liberal quests are shaped by existential beliefs. Also, the same is true in black religion where the point of christology is theology. For example, see *White Women's Christ and Black Women's Jesus: Feminist Christology and Womanist Response* (1989) by Jacquelyn Grant and *Encountering Jesus* (1992) by Zan W. Holmes Jr. For Grant and Holmes, "encountering Jesus" is about relationship to God, not about empirical-historical data.

6. While social ethics has explicit evaluative functions, social science is not without at least implicit evaluations. To be sure, merely selecting to be attentive to a given population is witness to valuing said population as worthy of selection. There is, then, no value-free social science. The possibility of a value-free social science is denied in Tony Smith's Habermasian account of social theory. In *The Role of Ethics in Social Theory: Essays From a Habermasian Perspective* (1991), Smith divides social theory into three general areas: social science, social ethics, and social policy. Regarding social science, Smith shows that, in contrast to Weber, Habermas's universalizability principle calls for "critical social science" rather than value-free social science.

7. The social ethical need to envision more righteous alternatives is emphasized in *O Lord, Move This Mountain: Racism and Christian Ethics* (1998) by E. Hammond Oglesby. Here Oglesby describes racism as a mountain, and he says the church needs "a vision beyond the mountain" (107).

8. Future-oriented accounts of ethics indebted to Whiteheadian metaphysics are presented in two other books: *Process Ethics* (1983) by James R. Gray, and *Moral Progress: A Process Critique of Macintyre* (2000) by Lisa Bellantoni. Gray holds that alongside "Process Theology," there should be a field of philosophical interest called "Process Ethics" (PE, 4). Drawing upon Whitehead, Gray displays a future-oriented account of ethics by saying: "Every individual shares a part of the responsibility for the shape of the future. The choices that we make in the present will help establish the nature of things to come. The future is open; awaiting the creative impact of all entities" (PE, 85). Similarly, a future-oriented Whiteheadian approach is offered by Bellantoni. Bellantoni argues that a Whiteheadian account of practical inquiry is more adequate than Alasdair MacIntyre's account. Where MacIntyre emphasizes the recapitulative function of narrative formed tradition, Bellantoni adds a

Whiteheadian emphasis upon tradition's creative function. Bellantoni holds Whiteheadian metaphysics implies that the primary task of practical enquiry is "not to reconstruct the past but to create the futures that that past envisions" (MP, 102). By soliciting future realizations of continually recreated and "distilled" ideals, practical inquiry serves moral progress. Also, see Peter C. Phan's *Culture Eschatology* (1985) and Linda L. Stinson's *Process and Conscience: Toward a Theology of Human Emergence* (1986).

9. Gamwell's account of the metaphysical necessity of God for moral theory is consistent with Ogden's account of the metaphysical implications of faith and justice. Ogden holds that faith demands justice, including political justice, and that faith and justice necessarily imply an unsurpassably just and all-inclusive individual—God. See Ogden's "The Metaphysics of Faith and Justice" in *Process Studies* 14.2 (Summer 1985), Special Issue on Liberation Theology, edited by Joseph A. Bracken, S.J.

10. Failure to recognize that understanding a part requires references to other parts and to the whole is a philosophical mistake that should be called "the Aesthetic Fallacy" because, says violin maker and sound theorist Duane Voskuil, "artists know that much of what colors or words do and mean come from the context they are in" (225). See Voskuil's "Hartshorne, God and Metaphysics: How the Cosmically Inclusive Personal Nexus and the World Interact," in *Process Studies* 28.3–4 (Fall-Winter 1999). Similarly, in the same issue, William Dean recognizes another strand of process thought indebted to John Dewey called "historical process theology," which holds that understanding a particular history requires references to other particular histories and to the whole of history. See Dean's "Historical Process Theology: A Field in a Map of Thought" where he says, "Dewey noted that any adequate understanding of one's history must refer to more than one's particular historical problems and include 'a sense of the whole' of history, and he called that sense of the whole the specific contribution of 'the religious' to a person's functioning" (261).

Epilogue

1. Drawing mothership connections reminds us that "the oppressed" were and are actual creative and interactive individuals and populations, not mere abstractions. That the poor are not mere abstractions is part of what Joerg Rieger means when, in *Remember the Poor* (1998), he says, "the poor . . . like 'the oppressed' or 'the marginalized,' do not exist as universals" (p. 4). Rieger's work in East Dallas, Jay Cole's work in central Dallas, Gloria Tate-Reed's work in Atlanta, and other social works with real people demonstrate that abstractions (such as "the poor" and "the oppressed") are seriously inadequate descriptions of actual individuals. Womanist theology is particularly attentive to making connections with actual individuals resisting oppression. For example, see Evelyn L. Parker's deliberations on Mrs. Fannie Lou Hamer

(1917–1977) and other individuals in "Twenty Seeds of Hope" (1996), in *Trouble Don't Last Always* (2003), and in *In Search of Wisdom: Faith Formation in the Black Church* (2002) edited by Parker and Anne E. Streaty Wimberly. Accordingly, bringing good news to the actual oppressed requires social analysis. See *Social Analysis: Linking Faith and Justice* (1983) by Joe Holland and Peter Henriot. Making connections with actual experiences of suffering from oppression reveals that oppression comes in various forms, and therefore the meaning of freedom from oppression is variable (Harding, TR). Hence, William Jones prescribes a "virus-vaccine" approach in which liberation struggle varies so as to resist ever mutating forms of oppression (IGWR, 206).

2. Overcoming patriarchy is emphasized in "Toward a Postpatriarchal Postmodernity" by Catherine Keller. Here Keller holds that "Feminism is a *conditio sine qua non,* a necessary if not sufficient condition, of any postmodern world" (SSPV, 74). Also, see Beardslee's "Men in the Post Patriarchal World" in *Creative Transformation* 8.2 (Winter 1998).

3. Whiteheadian and Hartshornean varieties of constructive postmodern theology are correctly described as revisionary or neoclassical because they offer revisions of classical theism. But like most varieties of postmodernism, they are not yet fully postmodern where postmodern is measured by reference to black Atlantic criteria for describing and transcending modernity. By black Atlantic criteria, Mark Twain/Samuel Langhorne Clemens (1835–1910) is more postmodern than most so-called postmodern writers. In *The Adventures of Huckleberry Finn* (1884), Twain is attentive to Mississippi River cargo, the experiences of slaves, and the struggle for freedom. Moreover, a liberating social ethic is indicated by Huck Finn's rejection of both law and classical theism in favor of liberty for a runaway slave. Here I am instructed by conversations with Juanita Walker Charles, Marvel Daniels, and Lillie Jenkins-Carter.

4. J. Deotis Roberts connects pneumatology with christology and liberation struggle in "The Holy Spirit and Liberation: A Black Perspective," in *A.M.E. Zion Quarterly Review* 96.4 (January 1985).

Appendix A

1. See "Metaphysics, History of" by Roger Hancock in *The Encyclopedia of Philosophy*.

2. When I speak of logically necessary existential truths, I am borrowing wording from Gamwell. Gamwell recognizes that there are claims about existence (existential claims) which are logically necessary—"logically necessary existential claims"—and that "the class of logically necessary existential claims is the class of valid metaphysical claims" (DG, 162).

3. Some so-called paranormal claims may turn out to be factually true. While the modern academic establishment tends to reject paranormal claims without serious attention to the evidence, some postmodern scholars argue

that an open-minded examination of the evidence supports some claims to extrasensory perception, psychokinesis, and other paranormal phenomena. For example, see *Parapsychology, Philosophy and Spirituality: A Postmodern Exploration* (1997) by Griffin. Also, see "The Paranormal Debate" by Douglas Todd in *Creative Transformation* 8.4 (Summer 1999): 21–22; and see Todd's review of Griffin's *Parapsychology, Philosophy and Spirituality* in this same issue (pp. 22–23).

4. Leibniz, as quoted in number 113 from page 138 of *Philosophers Speak of God* (University of Chicago Midway Reprint, 1976, originally 1953) by Hartshorne and William L. Reese.

5. Leibniz, as quoted in numbers 113 and 114 from page 138 of *Philosophers Speak of God*.

6. Leibniz, as quoted in number 113 from page 138 of *Philosophers Speak of God*.

7. The point of emphasizing "as such" is to distinguish between particular contingent realities and "reality as such" where "reality as such" refers to the noncontingent, unconditional, and necessary features of any actual or possible reality. Ogden and Gamwell speak of "reality as such." See Ogden in "The Criterion of Metaphysical Truth and the Senses of 'Metaphysics,'" in *Process Studies* 5.1 (Spring 1975), and Gamell in *The Divine Good* (158, 159, 165).

8. Most modern philosophical empiricism recognizes only publically verifiable *sensory* experiences. William James's radical empiricism recognizes a wider range of experiences. See *The Varieties of Religious Experience* (1902).

9. See "A Priori and A Posteriori" by D. W. Hamlyn in *The Encyclopedia of Philosophy*, and see "a priori and a posteriori" in *A Dictionary of Philosophy* by Antony Flew.

10. In *Hartshorne and Neoclassical Metaphysics* (1970) Eugene H. Peters says a metaphysical truth is "one whose denial results in incoherence," and this "negative test" for coherent denials is a "methodological key" for understanding Hartshorne's neoclassical metaphysics (16).

11. Some of Hartshorne's other formulations of the meaning of metaphysics include the following: "(a) The unrestrictive or completely general theory of concreteness; (b) The theory of experience as such; (c) The clarification of strictly universal conceptions; (d) The search for unconditionally necessary or eternal truths about existence; (e) The theory of objective modality; (f) The theory of possible world-states, or the a priori approach to cosmology; (g) The general theory of creativity; (h) The search for the common principle of structure and quality; (i) Ultimate or a priori axiology (theory of value in general); (j) The inquiry into the conceivability and existential status of infinity, perfection (unsurpassability), eternal and necessary existence; (k) The rational or secular approach to theology" (CSPM, 24). Hartshorne says these formulae "all imply the same thing and differ only in emphasis and focus of explicitness" (ibid.).

12. See Ogden's "The Criterion of Metaphysical Truth and the Senses of "Metaphysics" in *Process Studies* 5.1 (Spring 1975): 47–48.

13. Hartshorne recognizes the distinction between "human experience as such" and "experience as such." He says, "'Inherent in experience as such' means exactly what it says; 'inherent in human experience as such' would mean something else, and those who can see no great difference are probably not fitted for metaphysical inquiry" (CCSP, 25). Strict metaphysical claims apply to "experience as such," that is, to any experience, not just human experience. Hartshorne says metaphysical claims "are unique in applying to *any* experience, human, sub-human, super-human" (CSPM, 31). Similarly, Gamwell distinguishes between "pragmatically necessary" existential claims about human existence as such and "logically necessary" existential claims about existence or reality as such. Gamwell says that the study of "pragmatically necessary" existential claims is metaphysics "in the broad sense" and the study of "logically necessary" existential claims is metaphysics "in the strict sense," and that the broad sense of metaphysics is sometimes called "transcendental hermeneutics" and strict metaphysics is sometimes called "transcendental metaphysics" (DG, 160–63). Other terms for the broad sense of metaphysics include "speculative philosophy" (Whitehead, PR, 3), "speculative metaphysics," and "categorial metaphysics" (Ogden 1985, 100; EA, 35).

14. Gamwell speaks of "divine actuality." For instance, he says "the divine actuality" is "an all-inclusive relativity" (as in Hartshorne's *Divine Relativity*), and "all final real things" are "relativities" (DG, 169).

Appendix B

1. Theological focus on words and language, especially written language, contributes to characterizing "theology as grammar." In *An Invitation to Theological Study* (1994) Charles M. Wood shows how conceiving of theology as grammar can serve as "a useful characterization of the theological task in our own time" (98).

2. From Book One—"God"—of St. Thomas Aquinas' *Summa Theologica* as quoted in *Classics of Western Philosophy*, 4th edition (1995), edited by Steven M. Cahn (410–13).

3. The distinction between "zero-sum" and "non-zero-sum" games made by game theorists John von Neumann and Oskar Morgenstern is employed in *Nonzero: The Logic of Human Destiny* (1999) by Robert Wright. Wright argues that biological and human histories show a basic trajectory—evolution toward non-zero-sum interactions. Also, see Wright's website at <www.nonzero.org>.

4. Christian theology in the university includes a range of disciples. For a comprehensive orientation to the theological disciplines, see Wood's *Vision and Discernment: An Orientation in Theological Study* (1985).

5. See "An Evangelical Critique and Plan" by Walter C. Kaiser Jr. in *Theological Education* 32.1 (Autumn 1995): 68–69.

6. Abraham is critical of modern philosophical approaches to Christian theology in *Divine Revelation and the Limits of Historical Criticism* (1982), and in *Canon and Criterion: Christian Theology From the Fathers to Feminism* (1998). Also, for a theological deliberation on philosophy and a philosophical introduction to theology, see *A Philosophical Introduction to Theology* (1991) by J. Deotis Roberts.

7. See "On Keeping Theological Ethics Theological" (1983), "The Church as God's New Language" (1986), and other essays by Hauerwas reprinted in *The Hauerwas Reader* (2000), edited by Berkman and Cartwright.

8. Pedraja's conception of the divine *logos* as verbal and creative is consistent with Cobb's view of the divine *logos* as guiding the creative activity of the universe (CPA), and with Gamwell's view of the divine good as creative and variable—the "comprehensive variable" (DG, 168, 180–82).

9. Also, see *A Theology of Liberation* (1973) by Gutiérrez. Here Gutiérrez distinguishes between the classical task of theology as critical reflection on rational knowledge seeking "orthodoxy" and liberation theology's more inclusive understanding of the theological task as embracing critical reflection on both rational knowledge and historical praxis, including especially historical and contemporary churchly praxis, thereby seeking both "orthodoxy" and "orthopraxis" (TL, 10–15).

10. In "Theology in the University" (chapter 7) of *On Theology* (1986) Ogden holds that "Christian theology's standards of reflection are, indeed, the same in principle as those of any other field of study . . ." (OT, 131). Ogden destinguishes between "constructive philosophical theology" and "constructive Christian theology," and with regard to having a place in the university, Ogden holds that constructive philosophical theology "must have a place," and that constructive Christian theology has a place in an explicitly Christian university, but no necessary place in a secular university (OT, 129–31).

References

Abraham, William J. *Canon and Criterion: Christian Theology from the Fathers to Feminism.* London: Oxford University Press, 1998.

———. *Divine Revelation and the Limits of Historical Criticism.* London: Oxford University Press, 1982.

———. *The Logic of Evangelism.* Grand Rapids: Eerdmans, 1989.

Ali, Carroll A. Watkins. *Survival and Liberation: A Pastoral Theology in African American Context.* St. Louis: Chalice Press, 1999.

Allen, Joseph L. *Love and Conflict: A Covenantal Model of Christian Ethics.* Nashville: Abingdon, 1984.

Anderson, Victor. *Pragmatic Theology: Negotiating the Intersections of an American Philosophy of Religion and Public Theology.* SUNY series in Religion and American Public Life, ed. William D. Dean. Albany: State University of New York Press, 1998.

Asante, Kete, and Augusta Mann. *Activity Book for African American History: A Journey of Liberation.* Maywood, N.J.: Peoples Publishing Group, 1996.

Auxier, Randall E. "God, Process, and Persons: Charles Hartshorne and Personalism." *Process Studies* 27.3–4 (Fall-Winter 1998): 175–99.

Auxier, Randall, and Mark Davies, eds. *Hartshorne and Brightman on God, Process, and Persons: The Correspondence, 1922–1945.* Nashville: Vanderbilt University Press, 2000.

Baker-Fletcher, Garth Kasimu. *Dirty Hands: Christian Ethics in a Morally Ambiguous World.* Minneapolis: Fortress Press, 2000.

Baker-Fletcher, Karen. *A Singing Something: Womanist Reflections on Anna Julia Cooper.* New York: Crossroad, 1994.

———. *Sisters of Dust, Sisters of Spirit: A Creation-Centered Womanist Spirituality.* Minneapolis: Fortress Press, 1998.

Baker-Fletcher, Karen, and Garth Kasimu Baker-Fletcher. *My Sister, My Brother: Womanist and Xodus God-Talk.* Maryknoll, N.Y.: Orbis Books, 1997.

Baltazar, Eulalio P. *The Dark Center: A Process Theology of Blackness.* New York: Paulist Press, 1973.

Barbour, Floyd B., ed. *The Black Power Revolt.* New York: Collier Books, 1968.

Basinger, David. *Divine Power in Process Theism: A Philosophical Critique.* Albany: State University of New York Press, 1988.

Beardslee, William A. "Christ in the Postmodern Age: Reflections Inspired by Jean-Francois Lyotard." In *Varieties of Postmodern Theology.* SUNY series in Constructive Postmodern Thought, ed. David Ray Griffin. Albany: State University of New York Press, 1989.

———. "Cornel West's Postmodern Theology." In *Varieties of Postmodern Theology.* SUNY series in Constructive Postmodern Thought, ed. David Ray Griffin. Albany: State University of New York Press, 1989.

———. "Men in the Post Patriarchal World." *Creative Transformation* 8.2 (Winter 1998): 8–11.

Beckford, Robert. *Jesus Is Dread: Black Theology and Black Culture in Britain.* London: Darton, Longman, and Todd, 1998.

Bedini, Silvio A. "Benjamin Banneker, First Black Man of Science." *National Society of Black Engineers Journal,* Volume 3 (February 1988): 28–33.

———. *The Life of Benjamin Banneker: The First African-American Man of Science: Second Edition: Revised and Expanded.* Baltimore: Maryland Historical Society, 1999, first edited 1972.

Bellantoni, Lisa. *Moral Progress: A Process Critique of Macintyre.* SUNY series in Philosophy, ed. George R. Lucas Jr. Albany: State University of New York Press, 2000.

Berkman, John, and Michael G. Cartwright. *The Hauerwas Reader.* Durham: Duke University Press, 2000.

Bernal, Martin. *Black Athena: The Afroasiatic Roots of Classical Civilization, Volume 1: The Fabrication of Ancient Greece, 1785–1985.* New Brunswick: Rutgers University Press, 1987.

Blackburn, Robin. *The Making of New World Slavery: From the Baroque to the Modern, 1492–1800.* London: Verso Books, 1997.

Blassingame, John W., ed. *Slave Testimony: Two Centuries of Letters, Speeches, Interviews, and Autobiographies.* Baton Rouge and London: Louisiana State University Press, 1997 (originally 1977).

Bolster, W. Jeffrey. *Black Jacks: African American Seamen in the Age of Sail.* Cambridge and London: Harvard University Press, 1997.

Brown, Delwin. *To Set at Liberty: Christian Faith and Human Freedom.* Maryknoll, N.Y.: Orbis Books, 1981.

Browning, Douglas, ed. *Philosophers of Process.* New York: Random House, 1965.

Burrow, Rufus, Jr. *Personalism: A Critical Introduction.* St. Louis: Chalice Press, 1999.

Cahn, Steven M., ed. *Classics of Western Philosophy,* 4th ed. Indianapolis: Hackett, 1995.

Cannon, Katie Geneva. *Black Womanist Ethics.* American Academy of Religion Academy Series, ed. Susan Thistlethwaite. Atlanta: Scholars Press, 1988.

Carmichael, Stokely (Kwame Turé), and Charles V. Hamilton. *Black Power: The Politics of Liberation in America*. New York: Vintage Books, 1967.

Case-Winters, Ann. "Divine Perfection Reconsidered: Hartshorne's Innovation." *Creative Transformation* 6.2 (Winter 1997): 7–11, 35.

———. *God's Power: Traditional Understandings and Contemporary Challenges*. Philadelphia: Westminster John Knox Press, 1990.

Cerami, Charles A. *Benjamin Banneker: Surveyor, Astronomer, Publisher, Patriot*. New York: John Wiley and Sons, 2002.

Chapman, Mark L. *Christianity on Trail: African-American Religious Thought Before and After Black Power*. Maryknoll, N.Y.: Orbis Books, 1996.

Cobb, John B., Jr. *Christ in a Pluralistic Age*. Philadelphia: Westminster Press, 1975.

———. *The Earthist Challenge to Economism: A Theological Critique of the World Bank*. New York: St. Martin's Press, 1999.

———. *Postmodernism and Public Policy: Reframing Religion, Culture, Education, Sexuality, Class, Race, Politics, and the Economy*. Albany: State University of New York Press, 2002.

Cobb, John B., Jr., and Franklin I. Gamwell, eds. *Existence and Actuality: Conversations with Charles Hartshorne*. University of Chicago Press, 1984.

Cobb, John B., Jr., and David Ray Griffin. *Process Theology: An Introductory Exposition*. Philadelphia: Westminster Press, 1976.

Cobb, John B., Jr., and W. Widick Schroeder, eds. *Process Philosophy and Social Thought*. Chicago: Center for the Scientific Study of Religion, 1981.

Collins, Patricia Hill. *Black Feminist Thought: Knowledge, Consciousness, and the Politics of Empowerment*. Cambridge: Unwin Hyman, 1990.

Cone, James H. *Black Theology and Black Power*. New York: Seabury Press, 1969.

———. *A Black Theology of Liberation*. Philadelphia: Lippincott, 1970.

———. *God of the Oppressed*. New York: Seabury Press, 1975.

———. "The Origin of Black Theology." In *The Westminster Dictionary of Christian Theology*, ed. Alan Richardson and John Bowden. Philadelphia: Westminster Press, 1983.

Cousins, Ewart H., ed. *Process Theology: Basic Writings By the Key Thinkers of a Major Modern Movement*. New York: Newman Press, 1971.

Curran, Charles E. *The Church and Morality: An Ecumenical and Catholic Approach*. Minneapolis: Fortress Press, 1993.

Curtin, Philip. *The Atlantic Slave Trade: A Census*. Madison: University of Wisconsin Press, 1969.

Davaney, Sheila Greeve. *Divine Power: A Study of Karl Barth and Charles Hartshorne*. Cambridge: Harvard Dissertations in Religion Series, May 1986.

———. "God, Power and the Struggle for Liberation: A Feminist Contribution." In *Charles Hartshorne's Concept of God: Philosophical and Theological Responses*, ed. Santiago Sia. Dordrecht, Boston, and London: Kluwer Academic Publishers, 1990.

Davis, David Brion. *In the Image of God: Religion, Moral Values, and Our Heritage of Slavery.* New Haven: Yale University Press, 2001.

Dean, William. "Historical Process Theology: A Field in a Map of Thought." *Process Studies* 28.3–4 (Fall-Winter 1999): 255–66.

Dean, William, and Larry E. Axel. *The Size of God: The Theology of Bernard Loomer in Context.* Macon: Mercer University Press, 1987.

Deloria, Vine, Jr. *Custer Died for Your Sins: An Indian Manifesto.* Norman: University of Oklahoma Press, 1989 (originally 1969).

———. *God is Red: A Native View of Religion, Second Edition.* Golden, Colorado: North American Press, 1992 (originally 1973).

———. *The Metaphysics of Modern Existence.* New York: Harper and Row, 1979.

Deloria, Vine, Jr., and Clifford M. Lytle. *The Nations Within: The Past and Future of American Indian Sovereignty.* New York: Pantheon Books, 1984.

Devenish, Philip E. "Evil and Theism: An Analytical-Constructive Resolution of the So-called Problem of Evil." Ph.D. diss., Southern Methodist University Graduate Program in Religious Studies, 1977.

———. "Hartshorne's Eschatology: Gratefully Serving God." *Creative Transformation* 6.2 (Winter 1997): 17–18.

———. "Jews and Christians Searching for God." *America* 148.8 (26 February 1983): 144–52; reprinted in *Christian-Jewish Relations* 17.1 (March 1984): 13–19.

———. "Mind, Brain, and Dualism." *The Journal of Religion* 61.4 (October 1981): 422–27.

———. "Omnipotence, Creation, Perfection: Kenny and Aquinas on the Power and Action of God." *Modern Theology* 1.2 (January 1985): 105–17.

———. "The Sovereignty of Jesus and the Sovereignty of God." *Theology Today* 53.1 (April 1996): 63–73.

Devenish, Philip E., and George L. Goodwin, eds. *Witness and Existence: Essays in Honor of Schubert M. Ogden.* Chicago: University of Chicago Press, 1989.

Diop, Cheikh Anta. *The African Origins of Civilization: Myth or Reality.* New York: Lawrence Hill, 1974.

Dombrowski, Daniel A. Review of *Hartshorne and Brightman on God, Process, and Persons*, ed. Randall Auxier and Mark Davies. *Process Studies* 30.1 (Spring-Summer 2001): 166–68.

Douglas, Kelly Brown. *Sexuality and the Black Church: A Womanist Perspective.* Maryknoll, N.Y.: Orbis Books, 1999.

Douglass, Frederick. *My Bondage and My Freedom.* New York: Arno Press and The New York Times, 1969 (originally 1855).

Dow, George Francis. *Slave Ships and Slaving.* Salem: The Marine Research Society, 1927.

Du Bois, W. E. Burghardt. *Africa, Its Geography, People, and Products.* Ed. Herbert Aptheker. Millwood, N.Y.: Kraus-Thomson, 1977 (originally 1930).

———. *Africa—Its Place in Modern History.* Ed. Herbert Aptheker. Millwood, N.Y.: Kraus-Thomson, 1977 (originally 1930).

————. "Dusk of Dawn: An Essay Toward an Autobiography of a Race Concept" (1940). In *W. E. B. Du Bois: Writings*, ed. Nathan Huggins. New York: Viking Library of America, 1986.

————. *The Gift of Black Folk: Negroes in the Making of America*. Millwood, N.Y.: Kraus-Thomson, 1975 (originally 1924).

————. *The Souls of Black Folk: Essays and Sketches*. Nashville: Fisk University Press, 1979 (originally 1903).

————. *The Suppression of the African Slave-Trade in the United States of America, 1638–1870*. Cambridge: Harvard Historical Studies Series, Volume 1, 1896 (originally 1895 doctoral dissertation).

————. *The World and Africa: An Inquiry into the Part Which Africa Has Played in World History*. New York: Viking Press, 1947.

Dvorak, Katherine L. *An African-American Exodus: The Segregation of the Southern Churches*. Chicago Studies in the History of American Religion, Volume 4, 1991.

Earl, Riggins R., Jr. *Dark Symbols, Obscure Signs: God, Self, and Community in the Slave Mind*. Maryknoll, N.Y.: Orbis Books, 1993.

Edwards, Paul, ed. *The Encyclopedia of Philosophy*. New York: Macmillan, 1972 (originally 1967).

Erskine, Noel Leo. *Decolonizing Theology: A Caribbean Perspective*. Maryknoll, N.Y.: Orbis Books, 1981.

Esedeke, Effiong A. *Christians and Nigerian Politics*. Aba, Abia State: Effort Printers Nigeria, 2000.

Ferré, Frederick. *Being and Value: Toward a Constructive Postmodern Metaphysics*. Ed. David Ray Griffin. Albany: State University of New York Press, 1996.

————. "Toward a Postmodern Science and Technology." In *Spirituality and Society: Postmodern Visions*, ed. David Ray Griffin. Albany: State University of New York Press, 1988.

Finley, Moses I., ed. *Classical Slavery*. London: Frank Cass Publishers, 1999.

Flew, Antony. *A Dictionary of Philosophy*. Revised 2nd Edition. New York: St. Martin's Press, 1984 (originally 1979).

Gamwell, Franklin I. *The Divine Good: Modern Moral Theory and the Necessity of God*. Dallas: Southern Methodist University Press, 1996 (originally 1990).

Gilkes, Cheryl Townsend. "'A Conscious Connection to All That Is': *The Color Purple* as Subversive and Critical Ethnography." In *Embracing the Spirit: Womanist Perspectives on Hope, Salvation and Transformation*, ed. Emilie M. Townes. Maryknoll, N.Y.: Orbis Books, 1997.

Gilroy, Paul. *The Black Atlantic: Modernity and Double Consciousness*. Cambridge: Harvard University Press, 1993.

————. *There Ain't No Black in the Union Jack: The Cultural Politics of Race and Nation*. London: Hutchinson, 1987.

Githieya, Kimani. *The Freedom of the Spirit: African Indigenous Churches in Kenya*. Atlanta: Scholars Press, 1997.

Goatley, David Emmanuel. *Were You There? Godforsakenness In Slave Religion.* Maryknoll, N.Y.: Orbis Books, 1996.

Grant, Jacquelyn. *White Women's Christ and Black Women's Jesus: Feminist Christology and Womanist Response.* Atlanta: Scholars Press, 1989.

———. "Womanist Theology: Black Women's Experience as a Source for Doing Theology, with Special Reference to Christology." In *Black Theology: A Documentary History, Volume 2: 1980–1992,* ed. Gayraud S. Wilmore and James H. Cone. Maryknoll, N.Y.: Orbis Books, 1993.

Gray, James R. *Process Ethics.* Lanham, Md.: University Press of America, 1983.

Greene, Michael. "Peace and Justice!" *St. Luke "Community" Edition of the North Texas United Methodist Reporter* 5.28 (27 December 2002): 1.

Griffin, David Ray. *God and Religion in the Postmodern World: Essays in Postmodern Theology.* Albany: State University of New York Press, 1989.

———. *God, Power, and Evil: A Process Theodicy.* Philadelphia: Westminster Press, 1976.

———. *Parapsychology, Philosophy and Spirituality: A Postmodern Exploration.* Albany: State University of New York Press, 1997.

———. "Reconstructive Postmodern Theology." In *The Cambridge Companion to Postmodern Theology.* Ed. Kevin J. Vanhoozer. London: Cambridge University Press, 2003.

———. *Reenchantment Without Supernaturalism: A Process Philosophy of Religion.* Cornell Studies in the Philosophy of Religion. Ithaca: Cornell University Press, October 2000.

———. *Religion and Scientific Naturalism: Overcoming the Conflicts.* Albany: State University of New York Press, 2000.

———. "Values, Evil, and Liberation Theology." *Encounter* 40.1 (Winter 1979): 1–15. Reprinted in *Process Philosophy and Social Thought,* ed. John B. Cobb, Jr., and W. Widick Schroeder (Chicago: Center for the Scientific Study of Religion, 1981): 183–96. Also published as "Dios, el mal, los valores y la teologia de la liberacion" in *Praxis Christiana Y Produccion Teologica,* ed. Jorge V. Pixley and Jean-Pierr Bastian (Sallamanca, Spain: Ediciones Sigueme, 1978): 101–17.

———, ed. *Physics and the Ultimate Significance of Time: Bohm, Prigogine, and Process Philosophy.* Albany: State University of New York Press, 1986.

———. "Reconstructive Postmodern Theology." In *The Cambridge Companion to Postmodern Theology,* ed. Kevin J. Vanhoozer. London: Cambridge University Press, 2003.

———, ed. *The Reenchantment of Science: Postmodern Proposals.* Albany: State University of New York, 1988.

———, ed. *Spirituality and Society: Postmodern Visions.* Albany: State University of New York, 1988.

Griffin, David Ray, William A. Beardslee, and Joe Holland. *Varieties of Postmodern Theology.* Ed. David Ray Griffin. Albany: State University of New York Press, 1989.

Gutiérrez, Gustavo. *A Theology of Liberation: History, Politics, and Salvation.* Trans. and ed. Sister Caridad Inda and John Eagleson. Maryknoll, N.Y.: Orbis Books, 1973 (originally 1971).

Habermas, Jürgen. *The Philosophical Discourse of Modernity.* Cambridge: Polity Press, 1987.

———. *Postmodernism; Or, The Cultural Logic of Late Capitalism.* Durham: Duke University Press, 1991.

Hancock, Roger. "Metaphysics, History of." In *The Encyclopedia of Philosophy,* Volume 5, ed. Paul Edwards. New York: Macmillan and Free Press, 1972 (originally 1967).

Harding, Vincent. *There is a River: The Black Struggle for Freedom in America.* New York: Harcourt Brace Jovanovich, 1981.

Hartshorne, Charles. *Creative Synthesis and Philosophic Method.* New York: University Press of America, 1983 (originally 1970).

———. *The Darkness and the Light: A Philosopher Reflects Upon His Fortunate Career and Those Who Made It Possible.* Albany: State University of New York Press, 1990.

———. "The Development of Process Philosophy." In *Process Theology: Basic Writings By the Key Thinkers of a Major Modern Movement,* ed. Ewert H. Cousins. New York: Newman Press, 1971.

———. *The Divine Relativity: A Social Conception of God.* New Haven: Yale University Press, 1964 (originally 1948).

———. *The Logic of Perfection and Other Essays in Neoclassical Metaphysics.* LaSalle, Ill.: Open Court, 1962.

———. *Man's Vision of God and the Logic of Theism.* Hamden, Conn.: Archon Books, 1964 (originally 1941).

———. *A Natural Theology for Our Time.* La Salle, Ill.: Open Court, 1967.

———. *Omnipotence and Other Theological Mistakes.* Albany: State University of New York Press, 1984.

———. *Reality as Social Process: Studies in Metaphysics and Religion.* Boston: Beacon Press, 1953.

———. "Why Psychicalism? Comments on Keeling's and Shepherd's Criticisms." *Process Studies* 6.1 (Spring 1976): 67–72.

———. *Zero Fallacy and Other Essays in Neoclassical Philosophy,* ed. Mohammad Valady. LaSalle, Ill.: Open Court, 1997.

Hartshorne, Charles, and William L. Reese. *Philosophers Speak of God.* Chicago: University of Chicago Midway Reprint, 1976 (originally 1953).

Hauerwas, Stanley. "The Church as God's New Language" (1986). In *The Hauerwas Reader,* ed. John Berkman and Michael G. Cartwright. Durham: Duke University Press, 2000.

———. "On Keeping Theological Ethics Theological" (1983). In *The Hauerwas Reader,* ed. John Berkman and Michael G. Cartwright. Durham: Duke University Press, 2000.

Hayes, Diana L. "My Hope Is in the Lord: Transformation and Salvation in the African American Community." In *Embracing the Spirit: Womanist Perspectives on Hope, Salvation, and Transformation*, ed. Emilie M. Townes. Maryknoll, N.Y.: Orbis Books, 1997.

Hick, John. "Evil, The Problem of." *The Encyclopedia of Philosophy*, Volume 3, ed. Paul Edwards. New York: Macmillan, 1967.

Holland, Joe. "Christ in the Postmodern Age: Reflections Inspired by Jean-Francois Lyotard." In *Varieties of Postmodern Theology*. SUNY series in Constructive Postmodern Thought, ed. David Ray Griffin. Albany: State University of New York Press, 1989.

———. "The Cultural Vision of Pope John Paul II: Toward a Conservative/Liberal Postmodern Dialogue." In *Varieties of Postmodern Theology*. SUNY series in Constructive Postmodern Thought, ed. David Ray Griffin. Albany: State University of New York Press, 1989.

Holland, Joe, and Peter Henriot. *Social Analysis: Linking Faith and Justice*. Maryknoll, N.Y.: Orbis Books, 1983.

Holmes, Zan. W., Jr. *Encountering Jesus*. Nashville: Abingdon Press, 1992.

hooks, bell. *Feminist Theory: From Margin to Center*. Boston: South End Press, 1984.

Hopkins, Dwight N. *Down, Up, and Over: Slave Religion and Black Theology*. Minneapolis: Fortress Press, 2000.

———. *Introducing Black Theology of Liberation*. Maryknoll, N.Y.: Orbis Books, 1999.

Hopkins, Dwight N., and George C. L. Cummings, eds. *Cut Loose Your Stammering Tongue: Black Theology in the Slave Narratives*. Maryknoll, N.Y.: Orbis Books, 1991.

Ilesanmi, Simeon Olusegun. "Religious Pluralism and the State: A Socio-Ethical Study of the Religious Factor in Nigeria's Politics." Ph.D. diss., Southern Methodist University Graduate Program in Religious Studies, 1993.

James, George G. M. *Stolen Legacy*. San Francisco: Julian Richardson Associates, 1988 (originally 1954).

James, William. *The Varieties of Religious Experience: A Study in Human Nature*. New York: Penguin Classics, 1985 (originally 1902).

ben-Jochannan, Yosef A. A. *Africa: Mother of Western Civilization*. Baltimore: Black Classic Press, 1988 (originally New York: Alkebu-lan Books, 1981).

Johnson, Charles, Patricia Smith, and the WGBH Research Team. *Africans in America: America's Journey Through Slavery: Companion to the PBS Series*. New York: Harcourt Brace, 1998.

Jones, Major J. *Christian Ethics for Black Theology*. Nashville: Abingdon, 1974.

Jones, William R. *Is God A White Racist? A Preamble to Black Theology with a New Preface and Afterword*. Boston: Beacon Press, 1998 (originally 1973).

Just, Ernest Everett. *The Biology of the Cell Surface*. Philadelphia: Blakiston's, 1939.

Kaiser, Walter C., Jr. "An Evangelical Critique and Plan." *Theological Education* 32.1, Autumn 1995.

Kant, Immanuel. *Foundation of the Metaphysics of Morals.* Trans. Lewis White Beck. Indianapolis: Bobbs-Merrill, 1976 (originally 1785).

Keller, Catherine. "Toward a Postpatriarchal Postmodernity." In *Spirituality and Society: Postmodern Visions,* ed. David Ray Griffin. Albany: State University of New York Press, 1988.

King, Martin Luther, Jr. *Where Do We Go From Here: Chaos or Community?* Boston: Beacon Press, 1968.

Kirk-Duggan, Cheryl A. "Justified, Sanctified, and Redeemed: Blessed Expectation in Black Women's Blues and Gospels." In *Embracing the Spirit: Womanist Perspectives on Hope, Salvation and Transformation,* ed. Emilie M. Townes. Maryknoll, N.Y.: Orbis Books, 1997.

Lieb, Irwin C. *Experience, Existence, and the Good.* Carbondale: Southern Illinois University, 1961.

Lincoln, C. Eric, and Lawrence H. Mamiya. *The Black Church in the African American Experience.* Durham: Duke University Press, 1990.

Long, Charles H. *Alpha: The Myths of Creation.* Chica, Cal.: Scholars Press, 1963.

———. "Assessment and New Departures for a Study of Black Religion in the United States." *Chicago Theological Seminary Register* 21.1 (Winter, 1981): 4–16.

———. "The Black Reality: Toward a Theology of Freedom." *Criterion* 8.2 (Spring-Summer 1969): 2–7.

———. "Cargo Cults as Cultural Historical Phenomena." *Journal of the American Academy of Religion* 42.3 (September 1974): 403–14.

———. "Civil Rights—Civil Religion: Visible People and Invisible Religion." In *American Civil Religion,* ed. Russell E. Richey and Donald G. Jones. New York: Harper and Row, 1974.

———. "The Oppressive Element in Religion and the Religions of the Oppressed." *Harvard Theological Review* 69.3–4 (1976): 397–410.

———. "Perspectives for a Study of Afro-American Religion in the United States." *History of Religions* 11.1 (August 1971): 54–66.

———. "Primitive/Civilized: The Locus of a Problem." *History of Religions* 20.1–2 (August and November 1980): 43–61.

———. *Significations: Signs, Symbols, and Images in the Interpretation of Religion.* Philadelphia: Fortress Press, 1986.

———. "The West African High God: History and Religious Experience." *History of Religions* 3.2 (Winter 1964): 328–42.

———. "Why Africa Can't Be Dismissed as Merely Missionary Fodder: A Reply to Mr. Toynbee." *The Chicago Sunday Sun Times,* 12 February 1961, sec. 2, p. 3.

Long, Charles H., ed., with Joseph M. Kitagawa. *The History of Religions: Essays in Understanding.* Chicago: University of Chicago Press, 1967.

———. *Myths and Symbols: Essays in Honor of Mircea Eliade*. Chicago: University of Chicago Press, 1969.

Loomer, Bernard. "Two Conceptions of Power." *Process Studies* 6.1 (Spring 1976): 5–32.

Mamlyn, D. W. "A Priori and A Posteriori." *The Encyclopedia of Philosophy*, Volume 1. Ed. Paul Edwards. New York: Macmillan and Free Press, 1972 (originally 1967).

Manning, Kenneth R. *Black Apollo of Science: The Life of Ernest Everett Just*. New York: Oxford University Press, 1983.

May, William F. *The Physician's Covenant: Images of the Healer in Medical Ethics*. Philadelphia: Westminster Press, 1983.

Mesle, C. Robert. *Process Theology: A Basic Introduction*. St. Louis: Chalice Press, 1993.

McKissick, Floyd. *Three Fifths of a Man*. Toronto: Macmillan Press, 1969.

Middleton, Stephen, Charlotte Stokes et al. *The African American Experience: A History*. 2nd ed. Upper Saddle River, N.J.: Globe Fearon Educational Publisher, 1999.

Mitchell, Mozella. *The Spiritual Dynamics of Howard Thurman's Theology*. Bristol, Ind.: Wyndham Hall Press, 1985.

Moore, Mary Elizabeth Mullino. "Compassion and Hope: Theology Born of Action." In *Thy Nature and Thy Name Is Love: Wesleyan and Process Theologies in Dialogue*, ed. Bryan P. Stone and Thomas Jay Oord. Nashville: Kingswood Books, 2001.

Mostern, Kenneth. Review of *The Black Atlantic: Modernity and Double Consciousness* by Paul Gilroy (Cambridge: Harvard University Press, 1993) and *Framing the Margins: The Social Logic of Postmodern Culture* by Phillip Bryan (New York: Oxford University Press, 1994). <http://www.ctheory.com/r-modernity_postmodernity.html>.

Murphy, Larry G., ed. *Down By the Riverside: Readings in African American Religion (Religion, Race, and Ethnicity)*. New York University Press, 2000.

Neihardt, John G. *Black Elk Speaks: Being the Life Story of a Holy Man of the Oglala Sioux as Told Through John G. Neihardt (Flaming Rainbow)*. Lincoln: University of Nebraska Press, 1979 (originally 1932).

Newman, Richard. *Black Power and Black Religion: Essays and Reviews*. West Cornwall, Conn.: Locust Hill Press, 1987.

Ogden, Schubert M. "The Criterion of Metaphysical Truth and the Senses of "Metaphysics." *Process Studies* 5.1 (Spring 1975): 47–48.

———. "The Experience of God: Critical Reflections on Hartshorne's Theory of Analogy." In *Existence and Actuality: Conversations With Charles Hartshorne*, ed. John B. Cobb Jr. and Franklin I. Gamwell. Chicago: University of Chicago Press, 1984.

———. *Faith and Freedom: Toward a Theology of Liberation*. Nashville: Abingdon Press, 1979.

———. "The Metaphysics of Faith and Justice." *Process Studies* 14.2 (Summer 1985): 87–101.

———. *On Theology.* Dallas: Southern Methodist University Press, 1986.

———. *The Point of Christology.* Mexico City: Harper and Row, 1982.

Oglesby, E. Hammond. *O Lord, Move This Mountain: Racism and Christian Ethics.* St. Louis: Chalice Press, 1998.

Oord, Thomas Jay. "Wesleyan Theology, Boston Personalism, and Process Thought." In *Thy Nature and Thy Name Is Love: Wesleyan and Process Theologies in Dialogue,* ed. Bryan P. Stone and Thomas Jay Oord. Nashville: Kingswood Books, 2001.

Paris, Peter J. *The Spirituality of African Peoples: The Search for a Common Moral Discourse.* Minneapolis: Fortress Press, 1995.

Parker, Evelyn L. *Trouble Don't Last Always: Emancipatory Hope Among African American Adolescents.* Cleveland: Pilgrim Press, 2003.

———. "Twenty Seeds of Hope: Religious-Moral Values in African-American Adolescents in Chicago-land and Implications for Christian Education in the Black Church." Ph.D. diss., Garrett/Northwestern Program in Religious and Theological Studies, 1996.

Patterson, Sheron C. *New Faith: A Black Christian Woman's Guide to Reformation, Re-Creation, Rediscovery, Renaissance, Resurrection, and Revival.* Minneapolis: Fortress Press, 2000.

Pedraja, Luis G. *Jesus is My Uncle: Christology From a Hispanic Perspective.* Nashville: Abingdon Press, 1999.

Peters, Eugene H. *Hartshorne and Neoclassical Metaphysics: An Interpretation.* Lincoln: University of Nebraska Press, 1970.

———. "Methodology in the Metaphysics of Charles Hartshorne." In *Existence and Actuality: Conversations With Charles Hartshorne,* ed. John B. Cobb Jr. and Franklin I. Gamwell. Chicago: University of Chicago Press, 1984.

Phan, Peter C. *Culture Eschatology.* New York: Peter Lang, 1985.

———. "The Dipolar God and Latin American Liberation Theology." In *Charles Hartshorne's Concept of God: Philosophical and Theological Responses,* ed. Santiago Sia. Dordrecht, Boston, and London: Kluwer Academic Publishers, 1990.

Pinn, Anthony B. *By These Hands: A Documentary History of African American Humanism.* New York: New York University Press, 2001.

———. *Why Lord? Suffering and Evil in Black Theology.* New York: Continuum Press, 1995.

Pollard, Alton. *Mysticism and Social Change: The Social Witness of Howard Thurman.* New York: Peter Lang, 1992.

Rabaka, Reiland. "Deliberately Using the Word Colonial in a Much Broader Sense: W. E. B. Du Bois's Concept of 'Semi-Colonialism' as Critique of and Contribution to Postcolonialism." *Jouvert: Journal of Postcolonial Studies* 7.2 (Winter-Spring 2003). <social.chass.ncsu.edu/jouvert/v7i2/rabaka.htm>.

Reeves, Gene. "God and Creativity." *Southern Journal of Philosophy* (Winter 1969): 377–85.

Reid, Jennifer I. M., ed. *Religion and Global Culture: New Terrain in the Study of Religion and the Work of Charles H. Long.* Lanham, Md.: Lexington Books, 2002.

Rieger, Joerg. *God and the Excluded: Visions and Blindspots in Contemporary Theology.* Minneapolis: Fortress Press, 2001.

———. *Remember the Poor: The Challenge to Theology in the Twenty-First Century.* Harrisburg, Penn.: Trinity Press International, 1998.

Riggs, Marcia Y., ed. *Can I Get a Witness?: Prophetic Religious Voices of African American Women. An Anthology.* Maryknoll, N.Y.: Orbis Books, 1997.

Roberts, J. Deotis. "The Holy Spirit and Liberation: A Black Perspective." *A.M.E. Zion Quarterly Review* 96.4 (January 1985): 19–28.

———. *A Philosophical Introduction to Theology.* Philadelphia: Trinity Press, 1991.

Robinson, Randall. *The Debt: What America Owes to Blacks.* New York: Plume, 2000.

Sanders, Cheryl J. "Christian Ethics and Theology in Womanist Perspective." *The Journal of Feminist Studies in Religion* 5.2 (Fall 1989): 83–91; reprinted in *Black Theology: A Documentary History, Volume 2: 1980–1992,* ed. Gayraud S. Wilmore and James H. Cone. Maryknoll, N.Y.: Orbis Books, 1993.

———. *Empowerment Ethics for a Liberated People: A Path to African American Social Transformation.* Minneapolis: Fortress Press, 1995.

Scott, Kesho Yvonne. *The Habit of Surviving.* New York: Ballantine Books, 1991.

Sia, Santiago. *God in Process Thought: A Study in Charles Hartshorne's Concept of God.* Dordrecht, Boston, and Lancaster: Martinus Nijhoff, 1985.

———, ed. *Charles Hartshorne's Concept of God: Philosophical and Theological Responses.* Dordrecht, Boston, and London: Kluwer Academic Publishers, 1990.

Singleton, Harry H., III. *Black Theology and Ideology: Deideological Dimensions in the Theology of James H. Cone.* Collegeville, Minn.: Liturgical Press, 2002.

Smith, Abraham. "'There's More in the Text than That': William Wells Brown's *Clotel,* Slave Ideology, and Pauline Hermeneutics." In *1997 SBL Seminar Papers.* Atlanta: Scholars Press, 1997.

Smith, Archie, Jr. *The Relational Self: Ethics and Theory from a Black Church Perspective.* Nashville: Abingdon Press, 1982.

Smith, Luther. *Howard Thurman: The Mystic as Prophet.* Lanham, Md.: University Press of America, 1981.

Smith, Tony. *The Role of Ethics in Social Theory: Essays from a Habermasian Perspective.* SUNY Press Ethical Theory Series, ed. Robert B. Louden. Albany: State University of New York Press, 1991.

Spann, Thomas. "An Interpretation of an African-American Prayer." *The Journal of Religious Thought* 51.2 (Winter 1994-Spring 1995): 95–110.

Stinson, Linda L. *Process and Conscience: Toward a Theology of Human Emergence.* Lanham, Md.: University Press of America, 1986.

Sturm, Douglas. *Solidarity and Suffering: Toward a Politics of Relationality.* Albany: State University of New York Press, 1998.

Sutherland, Arthur. "The Motif of the Stranger in *The Souls of Black Folk.*" A paper presented at the Annual Meeting of the American Academy of Religion (Atlanta, November 2003).

Taylor, Charles. *Sources of the Self: The Making of Modern Identity.* Cambridge: Harvard University Press, 1989.

Terrell, JoAnne Marie. *Power in the Blood: The Cross in the African American Experience.* Maryknoll, N.Y.: Orbis Books, 1998.

Thandeka. *Learning to Be White: Money, Race, and God in America.* New York: Continuum Press, 1999.

Thomas, Hugh. *The Slave Trade: The Story of the Atlantic Slave Trade: 1440–1870.* New York: Simon and Schuster, 1997.

Thornhill, John. *Modernity: Christianity's Estranged Child Reconstructed.* Grand Rapids: Eerdmans, 2000.

Tilley, Terrence. *Postmodern Theologies: The Challenge of Religious Diversity.* Maryknoll, N.Y.: Orbis Books, 1995.

Todd, Douglas. "The Paranormal Debate." *Creative Transformation* 8.4 (Summer 1999): 21–22.

Townes, Emilie M., ed. *A Troubling in My Soul: Womanist Perspectives on Evil and Suffering.* Maryknoll, N.Y.: Orbis Books, 1993.

————, ed. *Embracing the Spirit: Womanist Perspectives on Hope, Salvation and Transformation.* Maryknoll, N.Y.: Orbis Books, 1997.

Townes, Mary M. "Looking to Your Tomorrows Today: North Carolina Central University, December 16, 1994." In *Embracing the Spirit: Womanist Perspectives on Hope, Salvation and Transformation,* ed. Emilie M. Townes. . Maryknoll, N.Y.: Orbis Books, 1997.

Trimiew, Darryl M. *God Bless the Child That's Got its Own: The Economic Rights Debate.* Atlanta: Scholars Press, 1997.

————. "The Renewal of Covenant and the Problem of Economic Rights: The Contributions of Daniel Elazar." *The Annual of the Society of Christian Ethics* 20 (2000): 105–09.

Voskuil, Duane. "Hartshorne, God and Metaphysics: How the Cosmically Inclusive Personal Nexus and the World Interact." *Process Studies* 28.3–4 (Fall-Winter, 1999).

Walker, Alice. *The Color Purple.* New York: Simon and Schuster, 1985 (originally Harcourt Brace Jovanovich, 1982).

————. *In Search of Our Mothers' Gardens: Womanist Prose.* San Diego: Harcourt Brace Jovanovich, 1983.

Walker, Corey D. B. "'Of the Coming of John [and Jane]': African American Intellectuals in Europe, 1888–1938." *Amerikastudien/American Studies* 47.1 (Spring 2002).

Walker, Theodore, Jr. *Empower the People: Social Ethics for the African-American Church.* Lincoln, Neb.: Authors Choice Press, 2001 (originally Maryknoll, N.Y.: Orbis Books, 1991).

———. "Theological Resources for a Black Neoclassical Social Ethics." *The Journal of Religious Thought* 45.2 (Winter-Spring 1989): 21–39; reprinted in *Black Theology: A Documentary History, Volume 2, 1980–1992*, ed. Gayraud S. Wilmore and James H. Cone. Maryknoll, N.Y.: Orbis Books, 1993.

Walls, Bishop William J. *The African Methodist Episcopal Zion Church: Reality of the Black Church*. Charlotte, N.C.: African Methodist Episcopal Zion Publishing House, 1974.

Wesley, John. "Thoughts Upon Slavery" (1774). In *The Works of John Wesley on Compact Disc*, ed. Thomas Jackson. Franklin, Tenn.: Providence House Publishers, 1995.

West, Cornel. *The American Evasion of Philosophy: A Genealogy of Pragmatism*. Madison: University of Wisconsin Press, 1989.

Westfall, Richard S., and Victor E. Thoren, eds. *Steps in the Scientific Tradition: Readings in the History of Science*. New York: John Wiley and Sons, 1968.

Whitehead, Alfred North. *Adventures of Ideas*. New York: Macmillan Free Press, 1967 (originally 1933).

———. *The Concept of Nature: Tarner Lectures Delivered in Trinity College November 1919*. London: Cambridge University Press, 1930.

———. *Essays in Science and Philosophy*. New York: Philosophical Library Press, 1947.

———. *Process and Reality: An Essay in Cosmology. 1927–1928 Gifford Lectures*, Corrected Edition, ed. David Ray Griffin and Donald W. Sherburne. New York: Free Press, 1979 (originally 1929).

———. *Science and the Modern World*. New York: Free Press, 1967 (originally 1925).

Wilkins, Roger. *Jefferson's Pillow: The Founding Fathers and the Dilemma of Black Patriotism*. Boston: Beacon Press, 2001.

Williams, Delores S. *Sisters in the Wilderness: The Challenge of Womanist God-Talk*. Maryknoll, N.Y.: Orbis Books, 1993.

Wilmore, Gayraud S. *Black Religion and Black Radicalism: An Interpretation of the Religious History of Afro-American People*. Maryknoll, N.Y.: Orbis Books, 1973.

———, ed. *African American Religious Studies: An Interdisciplinary Anthology*. Durham and London: Duke University Press, 1989.

Wilmore, Gayraud, and James H. Cone, eds. *Black Theology: A Documentary History, Volume 1, 1966–1979*, 2nd rev. ed. Maryknoll, N.Y.: Orbis Books, 1993 (originally 1979).

———, eds. *Black Theology: A Documentary History, Volume 2, 1980–1992*. Maryknoll, N.Y.: Orbis Books, 1993.

Wimberly, Anne E. Streaty, and Evelyn L. Parker, eds. *In Search of Wisdom: Faith Formation in the Black Church*. Nashville: Abingdon Press, 2002.

Wood, Charles M. *An Invitation to Theological Study*. Valley Forge, Penn.: Trinity Press International, 1994.

References

————. *Vision and Discernment: An Orientation in Theological Study*. Atlanta: Scholars Press, 1985.

Wright, Donald R. "Atlantic Slave Trade." *Microsoft Encarta Encyclopedia, 2000*.

Wright, Nathan, Jr. *Black Power and Urban Unrest: Creative Possibility*. New York: Hawthorne Press, 1967.

Wright, Robert. *Nonzero: The Logic of Human Destiny*. New York: Vintage Books, 1999.

Young, Henry James. *Process: A Theology of Social Pluralism*. Minneapolis: Fortress Press, 1990.

————. "Spirituality and Social Transformation: Perspectives on Wesleyan and Process Theologies." In *Thy Nature and Thy Name Is Love: Wesleyan and Process Theologies in Dialogue*, ed. Bryan P. Stone and Thomas Jay Oord. Nashville: Abingdon Press, 2001.

Young, Josiah Ulysses, III. *Black and African Theologies: Siblings or Distant Cousins?* Maryknoll, N.Y.: Orbis Books, 1986.

————. "Dogged Strength within the Veil: African-American Spirituality as a Literary Tradition." *The Journal of Religious Thought*, Volumes 55.2 and 56.1 (Fall-Spring 1999–2000): 87–107.

————. *A Pan-African Theology: Providence and the Legacies of the Ancestors*. Trenton, N.J.: Africa World Press, 1992.

Note on Supporting Center

This series is published under the auspices of the Center for Process Studies, a research organization affiliated with the Claremont School of Theology and Claremont Graduate University. It was founded in 1973 by John B. Cobb Jr., Founding Director, and David Ray Griffin, Executive Director; Marjorie Suchocki is now also a Co-Director. It encourages research and reflection on the process philosophy of Alfred North Whitehead, Charles Hartshorne, and related thinkers, and on the application and testing of this viewpoint in all areas of thought and practice. The center sponsors conferences, welcomes visiting scholars to use its library, and publishes a scholarly journal, *Process Studies*, and a newsletter, *Process Perspectives*. Located at 1325 North College, Claremont, CA 91711, it gratefully accepts (tax-deductible) contributions to support its work.

Index

a posteriori method, 75–76
a priori, 74, 78, 111n11
a priori method, 75–76
abolition of poverty, 104n3
abolitionism, 104n3
aboriginals, 69
Abraham, William J., 84, 113n6
absolute determinism, 55–59
ad hominem, 82
adolescents, African-American, 50–51
Aesthetic Fallacy, 109n10
Africa, 9–14, 20, 46, 90n1
African identity, 10–11
African Methodist Episcopal Church, 39
African Methodist Episcopal Zion Church, 38–39
A-ku, 11
Alexander, Samuel, 89n6
Ali, Carroll A. Watkins, 102n7
all-embracing love, 59–60
Allen, Joseph L., ix, 48–49
Allen, Richard, 39, 102n3
Allen Chapel African Methodist Episcopal Church, Roxboro, N.C., x
all-inclusive actuality, 79–80
all-inclusive good, 66–67

all-inclusive individual, 109n9
all-inclusive relativity (divine actuality, divine relativity, divine good), 112n14
all-inclusiveness, 31–33, 35, 66–67, 70, 79–80, 109n9, 112n14
almanacs, 16–18
American Academy of Religion, ix, 90n1
Amistad, 11, 92n8
analogical extension, 29, 100n10
analogy, Ogden on Hartshorne's theory of, 100n13
Anderson, Victor, 99n3
animals, 29
anthropology, 47
Antichrist, 37
antimodern movements, xi, xiv–xv, 4
antipatriarchal theology, 102n8
apartheid, xiv
Aquinas, Saint Thomas, 81, 83, 85, 112n2
Aristotle, 62, 73
Asante, Molefi Kete, 91n3
astronomy, 16–18, 89n6, 94–96n22–26
atoms, 30
Axel, Larry E., 107n8
axiology, 111n11

133

Bacon, Sir Francis, xii, 3, 7, 89n6
Baker-Fletcher, Garth Kasimu, 102n1, 103n11
Baker-Fletcher, Karen, 42, 48, 51, 103n11
Banneker, Benjamin, 16–18, 94–96n21–25
Banneker postage stamp, 96n25
Barbour, Floyd B., 105n1
Barnett, Ida B. Wells, 13, 93n13
Basinger, David, 106n5
Beardslee, William A., 4–5, 14–15, 88n4, 98n34, 110n2(Epilogue)
Beckford, Robert, 97n30
becoming, 28, 61–62, 66
becoming, process of, 28
Bedini, Silvio A., 95–96n24
being, "To be is to create" (CSPM, 1), 28
being, becoming, perishing, objective immortality, 61–63, 66
Bellantoni, Lisa, 108n8
Benezet, Anthony, 96n26
Ben-Jochannan, Yosef A. A., 97–98n33
Berdyaev, Nikolai, 28, 100n7
Bergson, Henri, 28, 87n2(Intro.), 89n6, 99n3, 100n7
Berkeley, George, 89n6
Berkman, John, 113n7
Berman, Marshall, 13
Bernal, Martin, 97–98n33
Bethel Church, Philadelphia, 39
Bethune-Cookman College, ix
Birch, Charles, 88n4
birth of modernity, 14–15, 25, 94n18, 98n35
black Atlantic, vii, 12, 15–16, 18, 20–21, 25, 45, 51, 69–70, 87n1(Preface), 92n11, 93–94n13, 97n31, 99n1, 110n3(Epilogue)
black Atlantic populations, vii
black church history, 38–40

black diaspora, 13, 97n30
Black Elk, 107n4
black experience as modern, 3, 12
black humanism, 40–41, 102n6
black liberation theology 26, 38, 40, 56, 70, 102n2, 102n7, 103–104n1
black nationalism, 37
black power, 37–40, 51, 53, 102n1–2, 105n1
"Black Power Statement," 38, 105n1
black empowerment theologies, 105n1
black sailors, 13, 93n12
black separatism, 37, 39
black theology, 9, 20–21, 26, 37–38, 40, 42, 45, 48, 51, 53–54, 57, 70, 90n1, 96–97n29–30, 102n2, 102n7, 103–104n1, 104n6, 105n2
black transatlantic travelers, 13, 93–94n13
Blackburn, Robin, 94n18, 98n35
Blassingame, John W., 11, 92n8
Bolster, W. Jeffrey, 93n12
Boston Personalism, 101n16
Boyle, Robert, 89n6
Bracken, Joseph A., 109n9
Bradley, Francis Herbert, 89n6
Brightman, Edgar Sheffield, 101n16
Brown, Delwin, 106n5
Brown, William Wells, 13, 93n13
Browning, Douglas, 99n3
Bruno, Giordano, 89n6
Burrow, Rufus, Jr., 101n16

Cahn, Steven M., 112n2
Cannon, Katie G., 103n10
cargo, 3, 9–12, 15, 16, 20, 70, 91n5, 94n19
Carmichael, Stokely (Kwame Turé), 37, 47, 104n2, 105n1
Cartwright, Michael G., 113n7
Case-Winters, Ann, 106n5, 107n7
categorical metaphysics, 112n13

Center for Process Studies, ix
Cerami, Charles A., 17, 94n21,
    95–96n23–25
Chapman, Mark L., 105n1
Christianity, 21, 98n36
christology, 84, 88n4, 104n5, 108n5,
    110n4
church history, 38–40, 102n2–5
circles of concern, 64–65
Civil Rights movement, 104n3
Civil War, 40, 104n3
Clark, Alvan, 94n22
classical theism, 33–34
classical dualism, 30, 42, 100n11
classical philosophy, 26, 33–34, 57
classical slavery, 16, 94n20
classical theism, 26, 33–34, 57–58,
    99n4
classism, 103n11
Clinton, George, x
Cobb, John B., Jr., 19–20, 88n4, 94n17,
    98n34, 113n8
collectives, 31, 100n12
Collins, Patricia Hill, 102n6, 105n1
colonialism, 18–19, 21, 56, 69, 92n7,
    98n34
completely restrictive existential
    statement, 77
comprehensive variable, 66
Comte, Auguste, 89n6
composites, 100n12
conciliar councils, 84
conditional necessity, 48–49, 51, 69
Cone, James H., 26, 37–38, 48, 51, 53,
    102n2, 103–104n1, 105n1
conflict and harmony, 48–49
constructive postmodern, 5, 14–16,
    87n2(Preface), 110n3(Epilogue)
contingency, 32, 45, 49, 53, 63, 66–67,
    69, 74–75, 111n7
contingent truth, 75–76, 78–79
Cooper, Anna Julia, 13, 48, 93n13
Copernicus, Nicolaus, 89n6

cosmology, 17–18, 111n11
Cousins, Ewert H., 99n3
covenant love, 48
creation, God of all creation, 25, 35,
    42, 51, 69–71
creative process, 27–28, 31, 35
creative synthesis, 28–29
creativity, 26–31, 35, 46–47, 63, 100n8,
    111n11, 113n8
creativity, "To be is to create"
    (CSPM, 1), 28
creativity, "universal of universals"
    (PR, 21), 28
Crummel, Alexander, 13, 93n13
Cummings, George C. L., 96n29
Curran, Charles E., 105–106n2
Curtin, Philip, 98n35

Darwin, Charles, 89n6
Davaney, Sheila Greeve, 106n5
Davis, David Brion, 90–91n2–3,
    94n18, 98n35
Dean, William, 107n8, 109n10
Declaration of Independence, 16
deconstruction, xii–xiii, 88n3(Intro.)
Delany, Martin Robinson, 13, 93n13
Deleuze, Gilles, xii, 87n2(Intro.)
Deloria, Vine, Jr., 21, 97n32
Derham, William, 95n23
Derrida, Jacques, xii, 87n2(Intro.),
    88n3(Intro.)
Descartes, René, xii, 3, 5, 7, 15, 89n6
descriptions, 64–65, 107n4
determinism, 55–59
Devenish, Philip E., 100n11, 105n10,
    106n5
Dewey, John, 99n3, 109n10
Dews, Peter, 88n3(Intro.)
Diop, Cheikh Anta, 97–98n33
discovery, colonial function, Deloria,
    21
discovery, method of discovery,
    Whitehead, 27

discrimination, 104n3
divine absolutes, 32–33
divine actuality, 101n18, 112n14
divine existence, 101n18
divine good, 66–67, 113n8
divine inspiration, 48, 70, 84, 104n5, 110n4
divine love, 59–60
divine relativity (surrelativism), 31–35, 66, 101n15, 101n17
divine revelation, 33–34, 84
Dogon people, 94–95n22, 96n25–26
Dombroski, Daniel A., 101n16
double consciousness, 12
Douglas, Kelly Brown, 102n9
Douglass, Frederick, 13, 38, 93n13
Dow, George Francis, 89–90n2
dual transcendence, 33–35
dualism, 19, 30, 42, 100n11
Du Bois, W. E. B., 12, 14–15, 17, 21, 93n13, 97n30, 97n33, 98n36
Du Bois's method (modernity by reference to slavery, Africa, double consciousness, color), 12, 14–16
Dvorak, Katherine L., 102n4

ecological destruction, 6, 18
economic rights debate, 91n5
economy, slave-trading free market, 3, 9–10, 21
Einstein, Albert, 89n6
empirical method, 75–76, 82
empiricism, 111n8
empowerment theologies, 105n1
Enlightenment, 13, 20
ephemeris, 16–17
epistemological certainty, 74
erotic liberty, 41, 102n8
eschatology, 105n10
Esedeke, Effiong A., 92n7
ethical deliberation, formal analysis of, 63–66, 70
ethics, 48, 61, 64, 66–67, 84

ethnic cleansing, 69
European technologies, 6
evangelism, 84
evangelizing, under divine inspiration, 70–71
events, all events, 33, 56, 61, 63, 64, 100n9
events, main events of modernity, 9, 14–15, 16, 25, 94n18, 96n27, 98n35
evil, xv, 53–54, 56–57, 106n3, 106n5
existence, 73–74, 76–78, 81
existence, nothing as nonsense, something as necessary, 73–74, 79
existential claims, 74–78, 110n2(Appendix A), 112n13
existential statements, restrictive and non-restrictive, 77–78
experience, 27–30, 51, 56–57, 62–64, 82, 84, 111n8, 112n13
experience as such, 79, 111n11, 112n13
extension, 61, analogical extension, 29, 100n10
extrasensory perception, 110–111n3

factual statements, 75–80
faith and justice, the metaphysics of, 109n9
fallacy of misplaced concreteness, 107n3
fallacy, zero, 30–31
falsifiability, 75, 77–79, 112n12
Fanon, Frantz, 93n13
feeling, 29–31, 62, 100n12, 105n10
feminism, xiii, 18, 102n6, 110n2(Epilogue)
feminist theology, 42
Ferré, Frederick, 6, 16, 19, 89–90n6–7, 94n16, 98n34
Finley, Moses I., 94n20
Flew, Antony, 111n9
Foucault, Michel, xii
Free African Society, 39

free market, 3, 9, 21
free trade, 9
freedom, 16–18, 30–31, 37, 40, 45–47, 50, 70, 103n1, 106n3
freedom fighters, 45
future, 62–66, 105n9–10

Galileo, Galilei, xii, 3, 5, 7, 15, 89n6
game theory, 112n3
Gamwell, Franklin I., 66, 74, 90n8, 99n2, 109n9, 110n2(Appendix A), 111n7, 112n13–14, 113n8
Garvey, Marcus, 13, 93n13
genocide, 69
ghosts, 74
Gilbert, William, 89n6
Gilkes, Cheryl Townsend, 41–42, 50, 104n8
Gilroy, Paul, 3, 12–14, 16, 87n1(Preface), 92n10–11, 93–94n12–15, 97n31
Gilroy's method (attention to ships, transatlantic travels, black Atlantic consciousness), 12–16, 92n10–11
Githieya, Francis Kimani, 102n5
Goatley, David Emmanuel, 96n29
God, 25, 27, 29, 31–35, 38, 41–42, 48, 50–51, 53–57, 59, 66, 69–70, 79, 81–85, 105n10, 106n4, 106n6, 109n9
God and ethics, 66–67
God of all creation, 25, 35, 38, 42, 51, 69–71
God of the oppressed, 25, 38, 42, 51, 69–71
good news, 70–71
gospel, 37, 70–71
Grant, Jacquelyn, 103n10, 108n5
Gray, James R., 108n8
Greek heritage, 16
Greek philosophy, 26, 99n4
Greene, Michael, 91–92n5

Griffin, David Ray, 3–4, 15, 16, 18–19, 21, 63, 87n2(Preface), 88n1–3, 100n9, 101n19, 106n5, 107n3, 110–111n3
Gutiérrez, Gustavo, 105–106n2, 113n9

Habermas, Jürgen, 13, 94n14, 108n6
Hamer, Fannie Lou, 109n1
Hamilton, Charles V., 37, 105n1
Hamlyn, D. W., 111n9
Hancock, Roger, 110n1
Harding, Vincent, 45–47, 109–110n1
Harper, Phillip Bryan, 94n15
Hartshorne, Charles, 4, 25–35, 46, 49, 51, 54–55, 57–58, 64, 66, 73–74, 76–78, 87n2(Intro.), 99n3–6, 100n8–10, 100–101n13–16, 101n18–19, 103n1, 104n7, 105n10, 106n3, 106–107n6–7, 110n3(Epilogue), 111n4, 111n10–11, 112n13–14
Hartshorne's method (consult experience, analogical extension, logical analysis of religious idea), 28–30, 31, 49, 64, 100n10, 100n14
Hauerwas, Stanley, 84, 113n7
Hayes, Diana L., 105n9
Hegel, George W. F., 89n6
Heidegger, Martin, xii, 87n2(Intro.)
Henriot, Peter, 109–110n1
Hick, John, 106n3
hip-hop music, 92n11
historical process theology, 109n10
history, 65, 97n33, 98n35
Hobbes, Thomas, 89n6
Holland, Joe, 4–6, 15, 20, 89n5, 109–110n1
Holmes, Zan W., Jr., 108n5
Holy Spirit, 48, 70, 84, 104n5, 110n4
Hood Theological Seminary, ix, 48
hooks, bell, 103n11
hope, womanist, 50

Hopkins, Dwight N., ix, 96n29, 102n2
Huggard, E. M., 106n3
humanism, black humanism, 40–41, 102n6
humanocentric theism, 40
Hurston, Zora Neale, 103n10
hypothetical necessity, 49

Ilesanmi, Simeon Olusegun, 92n7
imaginative generalization, 27
immortality, human, 33, 34, 62, 101–102n19–20, 107n2
immutability, divine, 33, 59
impassibility, divine, 34
imperialism, 4
individual, unique all-inclusive, 31–32, 34–35
individuals, 28, 30–31, 100n12, 106n4
infinity, 111n11
innate ideas, 74
integration, 40
interactivity, universal, 55–56
interpretive themes, 64–65

James, Cyril Lionel Robert, 93–94n13
James, George G. M., 97n33
James, William, 87n2(Intro.), 99n3, 111n8
Jefferson, Thomas, 16, 21
Jesus Christ, 37–38, 42, 71, 108n5
John Paul II (pope), 89n5
Johnson, Charles, 91n4
John Street Methodist Episcopal Church, New York City, 39
Jones, Absalom, 39
Jones, William R., 40, 56–57, 104n4, 109–110n1
Just, Ernest Everett, 96n26
justice, 45, 109n9

Kaiser, Walter C., Jr., 84, 113n5
Kant, Immanuel, 89n6, 107n1

Keller, Catherine, 110n2(Epilogue)
Kepler, Johannes, 89n6
King, Martin Luther, Jr., 37, 102n1, 104n3, 105n1
Kirk-Duggan, Cheryl A., 103n10
knowledge, 30, 74
Kristeva, Julia, xii

Leibniz, Gottfried Wilhelm von, 53–54, 75–76, 89n6, 106n3, 111n4–6
liberation struggle, 45–51
liberation theology, 18, 26, 38, 40, 42, 49, 56, 69–70, 102n2, 102n7, 103n1, 105n2, 106n5, 109n9, 113n9
liberty, 16–18, 30–31, 37, 40, 45–47, 50, 70, 103n1
Lieb, Irwin C., 99n6
linear power, 58
literature, 103n10, 110n3(Epilogue)
Livingstone College, 48
Locke, John, 74
logic, logical analysis, 6, 30, 33, 35, 74, 79, 82, 84
logically necessary existential truths, 26, 74–75, 110n2(Appendix A), 112n13
logos about theos, 81
logos as verbal and creative, 84–85, 113n8
Long, Charles H., 3, 9–10, 14, 16, 20, 90n1, 91–92n5–6, 92n9, 94n19, 97n30, 103n10
Long's method (attention to exchanges, including cargo, especially Middle Passage cargo), 9–16, 91–92n5–6
Long's publications, 90n1
Loomer, Bernard, 27, 58, 107n8
love, divine, 59–60, 66
love, human, 30, 59
Luddites, xi
Luke 4:18–19, 42, 70

Lyotard, Jean-Francois, 88n4
Lytle, Clifford M., 97n32

MacIntyre, Alasdair, 108n8
Malebranche, Nicolas, 89n6
man, 27, 29
Mann, Augusta, 91n3
Manning, Kenneth R., 96n26
many, "many become one" (PR, 21), 28
Marx, Karl, 89n6
Mason, George, 21
mathematics, 6, 74–75, 89n5
matter, vibratory theory of, 30
Maxwell, James Clerk, 89n6
May, William F., 107–108n4
McKissick, Floyd, 37
McMillan, Terry, 103n10
medical practice as social ethics, 107n4
medieval philosophy, 26
memory, 30
Mendi Land, 11
Mendi people, 11, 92n8
meta-ecology, 98n34
metaethics, 61, 66
metanarratives, xiii
metaphysica generalis, 79, 112n12
metaphysica specialis, 79, 112n12
metaphysical necessity, 49–51, 69, 75, 79, 109n9, 112n13
metaphysical truth(s), 64, 78–80, 111n10, 112n12
metaphysics, 26–27, 30–31, 45, 54, 61, 73–81, 99n2, 99n4, 100n13, 101n16, 103n1, 105–106n2, 109n9, 111–112n10–13
metaphysics, defined, 26, 73–79, 111–112n11–13
metaphysics of God, 31–32, 54, 66–67, 109n9
metaphysics of morals and values, 54, 61, 63–67, 107n1, 109n9

metaphysics of nature, 27–28, 61–63, 107n1
method of discovery, "like the flight of an aeroplane" (PR, 5), 27
Methodist Episcopal Church, 39
Middle Passage, 10–14, 20–21, 25, 90–91n2, 91n4, 92n6, 93n12, 94n19
Middle Passage, priority of, 10, 12, 20
Middleton, Stephen, 91n3
militarism, xiv, 4, 18
mind, 30–31, 100n11, 100n13
misplaced concreteness, 107n3
Mitchell, Mozella, 104n6
modern experience, 3, 12
modern identities, 11–12, 14
modern people, blacks as the first, 12
modern scientific civilization, 6
modern theism, 4
modern theology, 4, 20, 88n3 (chap.1)
modernism, xi–xii, 3, 70
modernity, xi–xv, 3–7, 9–10, 12, 16–18, 20–21, 25, 45, 56, 70, 84, 88n2, 89n5, 90n8, 92n6, 94n16, 96n27, 97n31, 98n34–35, 99n1
modernity, birth of, 14–15, 25, 94n18, 98n35
modernity, black Atlantic views, 3, 9–16, 20–21
modernity, main events, 9, 14–15, 16, 25, 94n18, 96n27, 98n35
modernity, marks (slavery, freedom, science, ignorance), 16–18
Moore, Mary Elizabeth, 99n5
modernity, postmodern views, 3–7, 14–16, 20–21
moral theory, 63–67
Morgenstern, Oskar, 112n3
Morrison, Toni, 103n10
Mostern, Kenneth, 94n15
Mother Bethel, Philadelphia, 39
"Mothership Connection," x

mothership connections, 25, 45, 70,
    109n1
Murphy, Larry G., 96–97n29
music, 92n11, 103n10

narrative, 108n8
Native Americans, 11–12, 21, 25,
    97n32
natural philosophy, 81
natural science, 73–75
natural theology, 106n4
nature, xii, xv, 18, 27, 29, 30, 48, 61,
    64, 73, 100n13
nature, metaphysics of, 27–31, 61–63
nature, transient aspect of,
    Whitehead, 61, 64
Nazi genocide, 6
necessary truth, 26, 46, 49, 66–67,
    74–77, 110n2(Appendix A), 112n13
necessity of God in ethics, 66–67
Neihardt, John G., 107n4
neoclassical antidualism, 42
neoclassical metaphysics, 25–27, 33,
    35, 45, 64, 66, 70, 104n7, 111n10
neoclassical philosophy, 26
neoclassical theism, 26, 33–34
neoclassical theology, 25–26, 33–34,
    54–58, 66, 110n3
neopragmatism, 87n2(Intro.)
Neumann, John von, 112n3
new age metaphysics, xii
Newman, Richard, 105n1
Newton, Sir Isaac, 3, 5, 7, 15, 89n6
Newtonian science, xii, 5, 15
Nigeria, 92n7
nihilism, xii
non-individual collectives, 31
non-restrictive existential statement,
    77–78
non-zero-sum game, 112n3
novelty, 63
nuclear destruction, 6
nuclearism, xiv, 4

objective immortality, 33, 34, 62,
    101–102n19–20, 107n2
observational falsifiability, 78, 112n12
Ogden, Schubert M., 34–35, 54–55,
    59, 78–79, 84, 99n2, 100n13,
    102n21, 103n1, 105n10, 108n5,
    109n9, 111n7, 112n12–13, 113n10
Oglesby, E. Hammond, 108n7
omnibenevolence, 53–54, 56–57
omnipotence, 26, 33, 35, 41, 53–54,
    56–57, 59–60, 107n7
omnipresence, 35, 70
omniscience, 32–35
one, "many become one" (PR, 21), 28
Oord, Thomas Jay, 101n16
oppression, 25, 38, 40–42, 45, 47–51,
    53–54, 69–71, 102n5, 109–110n1
organism, philosophy of, 28
orthodoxy, 85, 113n9
orthopraxis, 85, 113n9
Owens, William A., 92n8

panentheism, 31–32, 101n16
panexperientialism, 63, 100n9
panpsychism (psychicalism), 29–31,
    100n9–10, 100n12–13
pantemporalism, 63, 107n3
pantheism, 32, 101n16
paranormal claims, 74,
    110n3(Appendix A)
Paris, Peter J., 97n30
Parker, Evelyn L., 42, 50, 105n9,
    109n1
partially restrictive existential state-
    ment, 77–78
past, 62–64
patriarchal images of God, 41
patriarchy, xiii–xiv, 4, 41, 70, 102n8,
    110n2(Epilogue)
Patterson, Sheron C., 103n10
Pedraja, Luis G., 84–85, 103–104n1,
    113n8
peer review, 82–83

Peirce, Charles Sanders, 55, 87n2(Intro.), 99n3
perfection, divine, 33, 106n4, 107n7, 111n11
perishing, 62
Perkins School of Theology, 92n6, 94n19
personalism, 101n16
Peters, Eugene H., 49, 51, 104n7, 111n10
Phan, Peter C., 106n5, 108–109n8
philosophical theology, 81–85, 113n10
philosophy, defined, 81, 107n1
philosophy of nature, 107n1
philosophy of organism, 28
physicalism, xii, 87n2(Intro.)
physics, 30, 63, 73, 89n6
Pinn, Anthony B., 40–41, 102n6
Planck, Max, 30
Planck's constant, 30
pneumatology, 48, 104n5, 110n4. *See also* Holy Spirit
political concerns, 18
Pollard, Alton, 104n6
Popper, Sir Karl, 78
populations, 64–65
postmodernism, xii–xv, 3–7, 14–16, 18–21, 88n4, 98n34, 110n3(Epilogue)
postmodernity, xi–xii
postmodern theology, 4, 20–21, 25, 69–70, 88n3(chap.1)
poststructuralists, xiii
poverty, 6, 104n3
power, 30, 45, 53–54, 57–58, 70, 105–106n1–2, 106n5
power, linear, 58
power, persuasive not coercive, 106n5
power, relational, 58–59
power, shared, 58
pragmatically necessary existential truths, 26, 112n13

pragmatism, xii, 87n2(Intro.), 99n3
prayer, in African-American traditions, 105n10
predictions, 64–65, 107n4
prehension, 62
prescriptions, 64–65, 69
present, 62–64
process, 25–28, 46, 61, 99n2, 99n5, 101n16
process ethics, 108n8
process metaphysics, 64, 103n1
process philosophy, 26–27, 63, 99n3, 101n16, 103–104n1
process-relational thought, 99n5
process theology, 25, 98n34, 98n36, 99n3, 108n8
Protestantism, 41
psychicalism (panpsychism), 29–31, 100n9–10, 100n12–13
psychicalism, "applicable to all individuals whatever, from atoms to deity" (CSPM, 154), 30
psychokinesis, 110–111n3

Rabaka, Reiland, 98n34
race and class relations, 19
racism, 56, 103n11, 108n7
rationality, 82
reason, 81–82
reality as such, 74, 75, 111n7
reconstructive postmodernism, xiii–xv, 87n2(Preface)
Reese, William L., 111n4
Reeves, Gene, 100n8
Reid, Jennifer I. M., 90n1
relational power, 58–59
relations, 27, 99n5. *See also* social relations
relative determinism, 55–56
relativism, xii
relativity, 27, 99n5. *See also* divine relativity
relativity physics, 63

relativity, universal, 32
restrictive existential statement, 77
revelation, 33, 34
Rieger, Joerg, 99n1, 105–106n2, 109n1
Riggins, R. Earl, Jr., 96n29
Riggs, Marcia Y., 103n10
righteousness, 65–66, 69, 108n7
river metaphor, 46–47
Roberts, J. Deotis, 48, 104n5,
    110n3–4(Epilogue), 113n6
Robinson, Randall, 96n28
Roman heritage, 16
Roman Catholicism, 6, 41, 89n5,
    105n9, 105–106n2
Romanticists, xi
Rorty, Richard, 87n2(Intro.)

sailors, black, 13, 93n12
Sanders, Cheryl J., 41, 102n9, 105n1
science, xiii–xiv, 7, 16–17, 21, 73–74,
    94n16, 95n24, 96n26, 97n33
science, black Atlantic contributions,
    16–18, 95n24, 96n26, 97n33
Scott, Kesho Yvonne, 102n7
Scripture, 70, 82, 84, 103n10
secularization, 6
segregation, 102n4, 104n3
sentience, 30–31, 100n11, 100n13
separatism, 37, 39–40
sexual liberty, 41, 102n8
sexism, 103n11
sharing creativity, 26, 28–29
Shiloh Baptist Church, Greensboro,
    N. C., x
ships, especially slave ships, 9–11,
    13, 90–91n2–4, 92n8, 92n11, 93n12
Sia, Santiago, 100n14, 106n6
Sierra Leone, 11
Singleton, Harry H., III, 102n2
singulars, 100n12
Sioux nations, 21
Sirius, 17, 94n22
size of God, 107n8

slave religions, 20, 96–97n29
slave testimony, 11, 96n29
slavery, 9–16, 18–21, 25, 38, 40, 46–47,
    49, 53–54, 56, 69–70, 90–91n2–3,
    92n7, 92n11, 94n18, 94n20,
    96n26–29, 97n31, 98n35–36, 104n3,
    110n3(Epilogue)
Smith, Abraham, 96n29
Smith, Archie, Jr., 103–104n1
Smith, Luther, 104n6
Smith, Patricia, 91n4
Smith, Tony, 108n6
social conception of experience, uni-
    verse, God, 29, 31, 64
social ethics, 64–67, 69, 104n6, 107n4,
    108n6–7
social relations, 27–29, 31, 35, 64, 69,
    99n5
social science, 64–65, 108n6
Society of Christian Ethics, ix
Society for the Study of Black
    Religion, ix–x, 90n1
sociology, 64–65
Southern Methodist University, ix,
    104n2
Spann, Thomas, 105n10
special metaphysics, 79
special revelation, 34
speculative metaphysics, 112n13
speculative philosophy, 112n13
Spinoza, Benedictus, 89n6
St. George Methodist Episcopal
    Church, Philadelphia, 39
Stinson, Linda L., 108–109n8
St. Luke "Community" United
    Methodist Church, Dallas, Texas,
    x, 92n6, 94n19
Stokes, Charlotte, 91n3
strict metaphysics, 26, 45, 49–50, 51,
    69, 75, 79, 100n13, 112n13
struggle, 45–50, 70, 103n1, 104n3–4,
    110n3(Epilogue)
Sturm, Douglas, 99n5

subjective immortality, 33, 34, 62, 101–102n19–20, 107n2
surrelativism (divine relativity), 31–35, 66, 101n15, 101n17
survival, 102n7
Sutherland, Arthur, 93–94n13
sympathy, divine, 33

Taylor, Charles, 97n31
Teilhard de Chardin, Pierre, 40
temporal distinctions, 64
temporal process, 61–64, 107n2–3
Terrell, JoAnne Marie, 105n1
Thandeka, 19–20
theodicy, 53–54, 56–57, 106n3, 106n5
theology, defined, 81–85
theology in the university, 84, 113n10
Thomas Aquinas, Saint, 81, 83, 85, 112n2
Thomas, Hugh, 94n18, 98n35
Thoren, Victor E., 95n24
Thornhill, John, 97n31
Thurman, Howard, 48, 104n6
time, 13, 61–64, 107n2–3
timelessness in physics, 63, 107n3
Todd, Douglas, 110–111n3
totalitarian states, 6
Townes, Emilie M., 57–58, 103n10
Townes, Mary M., 50, 105n9
transatlantic slavery, 9–16, 18–21, 25, 38, 40, 46–47, 49, 53–54, 56, 69–70, 90–91n2–3, 92n7, 92n11, 94n18, 94n20, 96n26–29, 97n31, 98n35–36, 104n3, 110n3(Epilogue)
transatlantic slavery, August 1444 birth of modernity, 15, 94n18
transatlantic slavery, the numbers, 9, 90n2, 91n3
transatlantic travelers, black, 13, 93–94n13
transcendental hermeneutics, 99n2, 112n13

transcendental metaphysics, 99n2, 112n13
Trimiew, Darryl M., 91–92n5
truth, 26, 46, 49, 64, 66–67, 74–80, 110n2(Appendix A), 111n10, 112n12–13
Turé, Kwame (Stokely Carmichael), 37, 47, 104n2, 105n1
Twain, Mark (Samuel Langhorne Clemens), 110n3(Epilogue)

uncertainty, 73
unique all-inclusive individual, 31–32, 34–35, 55
universal acceptance, 59–60
universal action, 59–60
universal creativity, 27–29
universal good news, 70–71
universal interactivity, 34–35, 55–56, 106n4
universal of universals, 28. *See also* creativity
universal relativity, 32
universal sharing, 26, 28–29
university, 81–85, 112n4, 113n10
University of London, 12
University of North Carolina at Chapel Hill, 104n2
University of Notre Dame, 104n2

values, value judgments, 64–65
Varick, James, 39
verification, 75, 77
Vinci, Leonardo da, 89n6
visions, 64–65, 107n4
Voskuil, Duane, 109n10

Walker, Alice, 41, 50, 102–103n8–10
Walker, Corey D. B., 94n13
Walker, Theodore, Jr., 102n1, 103–104n1, 105n1
Walls, Bishop William J., 38
Washington, George, 21

Weiss, Paul, 99n6
Wesley, John, 96n26
Wesleyan theology, 101n16
West, Cornel, 88–89n4, 98n34, 99n3
Westfall, Richard S., 95n24
Wheatley, Phyllis, 13, 93n13
white identity, 11–12, 19–20
white supremacist theories, 21, 97n33
Whitehead, Alfred North, 4, 15, 25–29, 31, 34, 46, 61–65, 87n2(Intro), 88n4, 89n6, 96n27, 99n3, 99n5, 100n7, 100n9, 102n20, 103n1, 107n2, 108n8, 110n3(Epilogue), 112n13
Whitehead's method (science, observe experience, imaginative generalization), 15–16, 27–28, 31, 62–64
Wilkins, Roger, 19, 21
will, divine, 66
will, human, 30
Williams, Delores S., 102n7
Williams, Peter, 39

Wilmore, Gayraud S., 40, 102n2–3, 103–104n1
Wimberly, Anne E. Streaty, 109–110n1
win-lose scoring, 83
win-win scoring, 83
Wittgenstein, Ludwig, xii, 87n2(Intro.)
womanist theology, 41–42, 50, 57, 102n7, 103n9–12, 105n9, 109n1
Wood, Charles M., ix, 95n23, 112n1, 112n4
World War, 5, 6, 20
Wright, Donald R., 91n3–4
Wright, Nathan, Jr., 105n1
Wright, Richard, 13, 93n13
Wright, Robert, 112n3

Young, Henry James, 21, 98n36, 103–104n1
Young, Josiah, 97n30

zero fallacy, 30–31
zero-sum game, 83, 112n3
Zion Church, 39

SUNY series in Constructive Postmodern Thought
David Ray Griffin, series editor

David Ray Griffin, editor, *The Reenchantment of Science: Postmodern Proposals*

David Ray Griffin, editor, *Spirituality and Society: Postmodern Visions*

David Ray Griffin, *God and Religion in the Postmodern World: Essays in Postmodern Theology*

David Ray Griffin, William A. Beardslee, and Joe Holland, *Varieties of Postmodern Theology*

David Ray Griffin and Huston Smith, *Primordial Truth and Postmodern Theology*

David Ray Griffin, editor, *Sacred Interconnections: Postmodern Spirituality, Political Economy, and Art*

Robert Inchausti, *The Ignorant Perfection of Ordinary People*

David W. Orr, *Ecological Literacy: Education and the Transition to a Postmodern World*

David Ray Griffin, John B. Cobb Jr., Marcus P. Ford, Pete A. Y. Gunter, and Peter Ochs, *Founders of Constructive Postmodern Philosophy: Peirce, James, Bergson, Whitehead, and Hartshorne*

David Ray Griffin and Richard A. Falk, editors, *Postmodern Politics for a Planet in Crisis: Policy, Process, and Presidential Vision*

Steve Odin, *The Social Self in Zen and American Pragmatism*

Frederick Ferré, *Being and Value: Toward a Constructive Postmodern Metaphysics*

Sandra B. Lubarsky and David Ray Griffin, editors, *Jewish Theology and Process Thought*

J. Baird Callicott and Fernando J. R. da Rocha, editors, *Earth Summit Ethics: Toward a Reconstructive Postmodern Philosophy of Environmental Education*

David Ray Griffin, *Parapsychology, Philosophy, and Spirituality: A Postmodern Exploration*

Jay Earley, *Transforming Human Culture: Social Evolution and the Planetary Crisis*

Daniel A. Dombrowski, *Kazantzakis and God*

E. M. Adams, *A Society Fit for Human Beings*

Frederick Ferré, *Knowing and Value: Toward a Constructive Postmodern Epistemology*

Jerry H. Gill, *The Tacit Mode: Michael Polanyi's Postmodern Philosophy*

Nicholas F. Gier, *Spiritual Titanism: Indian, Chinese, and Western Perspectives*

David Ray Griffin, *Religion and Scientific Naturalism: Overcoming the Conflicts*

John A. Jungerman, *World in Process: Creativity and Interconnection in the New Physics*

Frederick Ferré, *Living and Value: Toward a Constructive Postmodern Ethics*

Laurence Foss, *The End of Modern Medicine: Biomedical Science Under a Microscope*

John B. Cobb Jr., *Postmodernism and Public Policy: Reframing Religion, Culture, Education, Sexuality, Class, Race, Politics, and the Economy*

Catherine Keller and Anne Daniell, editors, *Process and Difference: Between Cosmological and Poststructuralist Postmodernisms*

Timothy E. Eastman and Hank Keeton, editors, *Physics and Whitehead: Quantum, Process, and Experience*

Nicholas F. Gier, *The Virtue of Nonviolence: From Gautama to Gandhi*

George Allan, *Higher Education in the Making: Pragmatism, Whitehead, and the Canon*